How To Make Christmas Ornaments

How To Make Christmas Ornaments

By Harryette S. Hendricks

Country Beautiful Corporation
Waukesha, Wisconsin

ACKNOWLEDGEMENT

Had it not been for the insistence of
Oleg Kay that I share this pleasure
with others, this book would not have
been written.

COUNTRY BEAUTIFUL: *Publisher and Editorial Director:* Michael P.
Dineen; *Executive Editor:* Robert L. Polley; *Senior Editors:* Kenneth L.
Schmitz, James H. Robb; *Art Director:* Buford Nixon; *Associate Editors:*
D'Arlyn M. Marks, John M. Nuhn; *Editorial Assistants:* Nancy Backes, Kay
Kundinger; *Production Manager:* Donna Griesemer; *Art Assistant:* Tom
McCann; *Editorial Secretary:* Jane Boyd; *Administration:* Brett Gries; *Staff:*
Bruce Schneider.

Country Beautiful Corporation is a wholly owned subsidiary
of Flick-Reedy Corporation: President: Frank Flick; Vice
President and General Manager: Michael P. Dineen; Treasurer
and Secretary: August Caamano.

*Frontispiece: A Christmas tree decorated with all the
ornaments described in this book.*

CONTENTS

Introduction: How I Got Started

Decorating for holidays with your own creations is a fascinating and gratifying hobby. I am told that $10.5 billion is spent yearly on hobbies in the United States: golf, fishing, sailing, candlemaking, ceramics, wood-working, novelties in papier-maché, needlepoint, bowling, crewel embroidery, painting, travel, photography, music, knitting, refinishing furniture, taking courses in this or that. They allow all our pent-up artistry and energy to express themselves. And this expenditure of time and money has been brought about because of our increased longevity, our increased affluence, and our increased hours of free time which we want to use both pleasurably and profitably. Who among us wants to sit and stare?

Certainly it has happened that the great numbers of us who have taken up a new hobby have witnessed the creativity within ourselves. This ability to create was there all the while but unknown because it was unexpressed. Some of us make lamps out of driftwood; candlesticks out of decorated orange juice cans; jewel boxes out of toolboxes; flower vases out of cut-off curvacious wine bottles; pictures out of seeds or seashells; animals out of pine cones. There is a person on Cape Cod who weaves purses in the form of a basket. Price: $150.00.

You, too, are creative. Show it! Show it not one-of-these-days, but now!

Creating holiday decorations, such as will be suggested in this book, is a soul-satisfying hobby which expresses your complete self. They show what your brain and very own hands can produce; and as you and family and friends contemplate your creations, you can say to yourself without immodesty: "It's all my own doing, my own ideas of color, scale, design, contrasts, and harmonies!" No pleasure compares with seeing come to life your own innate creativity. The process of expressing it will not only delight you, it will astonish you!

I am often asked just what it was that impelled me toward this sensuous gratification of making the decorations described in this book. The answer is: I honestly don't know that it was any *one* reason. Maybe it was "sun spots." Maybe it was the desire to have an interlude, a changeover from the workaday world of pushing a carpet sweeper or waxing machine, of bringing in the victuals, of doing the laundry, of polishing the silver and copper and brass, of annihilating the grime from pictures and mirrors, of weeding and raking and fertilizing and pruning — all necessary jobs, indeed, but all of them nothing more than manual labor. Productive but uninspiring.

But when I scrutinize the situation, I think that the *real* reason for embarking on this hobby was simply a desire of mine to "build a better mousetrap": A friend gave me a present of a decorated Christmas ball. It was colorful and pretty, covered with variously shaped sequins pinned to a styrofoam ball. Upon closer look, I thought to myself: "It's Christmas-y all right, but wouldn't it be possible to do better than that — to give it some oomph, some individuality, some pizazz, and end up making it really jewellike?"

I thought at once of ribbons and braids, of velvets and satins, of silken tassels, and of no-longer-used costume jewelry which was wasting away in my jewelry boxes. And after the Christmas cleanup was over and the post-season lull and liberty set in, I began to experiment. My goal was to produce something fabulously beautiful, and I pursued this goal as if I were killing snakes. One idea led to another, and the urge to execute still another became so insistent that, if I awoke at three or four o'clock in the morning, instead of going back to sleep, I felt positively compelled to go downstairs and enjoy myself with my decorations. The eleventh became prettier than the tenth, the twelfth prettier than the eleventh, and so on!

I soon found myself hooked on, obsessed by, addicted to my newfound pleasure. Addicted not to what should be stopped, but addicted to what I should *start*! And having pointed myself in this direction, nothing was to veer me off my course. If my husband awoke and found me not in our

bedroom, he'd go downstairs to admonish me: "You're ruining your health. You're not getting enough rest. Come go to sleep." But I persevered at my pleasure until the household was awake and ready for breakfast.

"You must be awfully tired," he'd say.

"Tired? Not a bit of it. Feel great!"

"Sleepy then, I know," and as he went out of the door for his office, he tried cajoling me: "Can't you stop with your decorations for a few hours? I realize that you're very gung-ho about your decorations. But I wish you'd leave them for a few hours, take a sleeping pill, and lie down awhile."

I never did. No, never once did I take that pill. I had no tired blood!

Now take a look at some of the commercially made Christmas decorations or those made by friends with Tender-Loving-Care; and you will be saying to yourself: "I, too, can do better than that." You will say this even though you may think that you have no artistic bent and that you aren't good with your hands. Set out! Take the step! We learn to do by doing. The more you proceed, the more ideas you'll come up with, impatient to finish the one you're working on in order to begin the next, each with a different concept, using differing materials, differing color combinations, some of them classical, some psychedelic, some dainty, some bold.

There is no limit to the ways in which you can decorate glamorously with these "glittering fragments of the rainbow." Besides suspending them on your tree, fill a bowl with them for your foyer table; hang them on a wrought-iron candleholder or on a silver candelabrum as a centerpiece for your holiday table; suspend them from your chandeliers; put them here and there on pine branches on your mantel or on a rope of pine entwined on the railing of your stairway; make eardrops from the tiny ones; wall plaques; a wreath for your entrance door; put one at each dinner place for your family and holiday guests. Why not pin the name of the recipient on each as a place card? You'll find a dozen more ways to use them for embellishing your holidays. (See Chapter "Other Ways, Other Uses" for details.)

They are very simple to make, yet challenging, and they have the added advantage of being non-breakable and non-perishable. You'll use them year after year and experience anew the exhilaration of contemplating your own artistry.

Now that I live alone, I no longer bother with putting up and taking down a Christmas tree, yet my apartment is not only "Christmas-y," it is quite charming and indeed distinctive because no one, but no one, has the selfsame décor. There is the festivity of the holidays in every room minus the fuss of getting the tree set up and taken down. The customary after-Christmas cleaning up and clearing out is happily limited to stashing away the decorations into a box until next year.

If selling your creations is what you want to do, start out with eardrops. To convince yourself of your potential, try the following: Decorate two tiny styrofoam balls (see the Chapter "Now Decorate Yourself") and hang them on a pair of your eardrops. They will make even the most conservative costume into something eye-catching and way out.

The first time I wore a pair to a party at Christmastime, some of the guests — males as well as females (Is Kinsey right? Who knows exactly what's going on behind our female backs?) — demanded, despite my protestations of Christmas busy-ness, that I make as many as possible for their gift giving. So, a brief warning: Unless you want to make eardrops in quantity, don't wear them except in the privacy of your own home. Because it's rude to reply to a request with a flat "No."

If you can withstand the emotional tug of parting with your creations, you have lots of ready-made markets: Sell them at a nice profit to any of the stores which have a snazzy Christmas boutique. But if money doesn't interest you, donate them to a fund-raising sale which your church or club or some charitable organization may be sponsoring. The tax write-off for the donation will be quite welcome the following April! Or decorate a hospital waiting room, or put a glamorous bowl of them in a senior citizens' living room, or dress up the entrance of a correctional institution.

Those interested in selling their creations would find interesting the story of how I became, with no effort on my part, a yearly supplier to three swank New York stores. A friend of mine used them as the centerpiece for his Christmas dinner table. Among the guests for the dinner was the buyer for a Christmas boutique. The buyer-friend told him: "Henry, these are great. They remind me of the decorations on the Christmas tree in *The Nutcracker Suite*. Get me in touch with the maker." Henry called me and told me to take a dozen or so of them into New York to show to the buyer at Georg Jensen.

I told Henry: "No, I don't want to do that . . . because I've never sold anything. I don't know how to sell."

He insisted, but so did I.

In a few days, he called me: "Surprise! I took the decorations, the ones that you gave me, into New York. You have an order for a gross. He wants them by August 15th."

"A gross! That's 144, isn't it? Heavens to Betsy, I can't make that many. I have lots to do apart from making Christmas decorations: a husband, the children, three dogs, the garden. No, Henry, impossible!" Although I was flattered, I was bowled over by the enormity of it.

But he wouldn't quit. I remember that he tried enticing me by uttering such thoughts as: "The back is made to fit the burden" and "God tempers the wind to the shorn lamb." But I refused to budge. "Tell your buyer-friend at Jensen's to forget the whole bit."

"No, I won't!" Long pause. A very long pause. "Tell you what I'll do," he burst out, "*I'll* help you with the order."

"*You* help? How could *you* help? You don't know how to make them!"

Henry: "I'll cover the styrofoam with the cloths. *Anyone* can do that, and that'll be a help, won't it?"

He came over, got the styrofoam and fabrics, and returned periodically with dozens covered. The 144 were finished. This never-say-die character took them to New York in his station wagon and returned with a fat check. Filling that order was a real achievement for me, and the money seemed like pure gold!

Word got around, as words do, and I soon had a very lively business going. Altogether unsolicited. Not only did the boutiques buy the decorations to sell, they used them to decorate their own boutiques as well as show windows. One December night, my daughter (then fifteen), her escort, and I were walking along Fifth Avenue on our way to a party at the Plaza Hotel. From time to time, we paused to admire the glamorous displays in the stores' display windows. As you know, in order to reach the Plaza, one must pass Bergdorf Goodman; and my daughter, upon seeing my decorations revolving slowly on an invisible Christmas tree, blurted out, for all the Fifth Avenue crowd to hear: "Look, Tim! Look! There are my mother's *balls!*"

What You'll Need and Where to Get It

Many of the things you'll be needing you already have: a pair of scissors, Elmer's glue, ordinary straight pins as well as sequin pins (they're the tiny ones and come in "gold" as well as in "silver") and corsage pins, round toothpicks, pliers, an ice pick, several sizes of small brushes, fine wire, floral wire, and small wire cutters. These are the tools of your trade-to-be.

As to the materials for the decorating, you'll be gathering ribbons, laces, costume jewelry you've grown tired of (or maybe it's no longer in vogue), hairpins, sequins (various colors of single ones as well as the rope sequins), discarded skirts, blouses, dresses, or perhaps an old evening coat. I well remember a white lace dress that had a gold thread which outlined the flower design. How I adored that evening dress, complete with train! I over-wore it until I finally arrived at the sad conclusion that because it had been seen so often I would either have to discard the dress from my wardrobe or change my friends. Yet I couldn't part with it completely. So I packed it carefully and stowed it in the attic — only to bring it out thirty years later to serve me again, this time *not* on the dance floor while imagining myself Irene Castle, but in my newfound hobby which occupied me for fun and for profit.

Take a look at your clothes. Go through your closet piece by piece. It may seem a bit drastic, but a good rule to follow on discarding clothes is: If you haven't worn it in two years, you probably never will. What about an old felt skirt or jacket? Also a velvet dress or coat that once were really "smashing" but no more?

Now pull out your scrap bag. Is there a piece of mohair in there (mohair cloth is easy to work with because it doesn't show seams), or a bit of satin, or a gay print, or maybe even some lamé? If you don't hoard favorite old clothes nor have a scrap bag, go out and get a few attractive remnants for little or nothing.

The cloths which you will be using for covering the styrofoam as well as the "jewels," braids, ribbons, roping, etc., can be found in "outlet stores," fabric stores, notions departments, and in little out-of-the-way places which deal in just about everything in the way of novelties. But the most fun of all is obtaining your materials at thrift shops, rummage sales, white elephant sales, tag sales, barn sales, garage sales — euphemisms, all, for "junk sales"; but even with these many different names, they're all roses which smell sweet. They'll supply you with undreamed-of treasures.

So, poke around, snoop around. You could even ask your friends for "junk" which they'd be glad to get rid of, particularly costume jewelry. And what at first glance may seem ridiculous will turn out to be just the ticket

for your ultimate purpose. You will discover that often you'll be "making something out of nothing," a feat which gives real satisfaction. For example, a nothing could be a necklace made of seashells. Are these unlikely candidates for your needed decorations? No! You will see that you'll be using them in a dozen different ways. Or you may, in your rounds, come across a charm bracelet made of various animals of the sea (a lobster, a clam, a sea horse, a starfish). These would be appropriate for your gift to a fisherman friend or for the boating enthusiast. Hearts abound in all shapes and designs. These you'll be putting on your gifts for those near and dear to you. In your Sherlock Holmes-ing, you may happen upon a bracelet from which dangle spades, hearts, diamonds, and clubs. These would be a gas for your gifts to your poker-playing or bridge-playing friends. The list is endless, once your imagination is in high gear.

I can recount a couple of incidents about finding unlikely candidates for my decorations in unlikely places. The decoration on "Kings of the Realm" V comes to mind. An elderly neighbor of mine had cleaned out her attic and left the debris in a big box to be picked up by the city's clean-up campaign. I saw on the top of the pile a pair of silver leather shoes. (I remember that in the dear, dead days of long, long ago my mother had similar ones.) The neighbor's had thongs which came up over the instep and buttoned on the sides of the shoe. In the thong was a hexagonal setting of rhinestones.

I rang her bell. "Dora, could I take those silver shoes from your junk heap on the sidewalk?"

She looked a little puzzled and then laughed. "Sure, my dear. But they're so out-of-date! I've had them for forty years." A nostalgic look came over her face. "You're not going to wear them, are you?"

"Hardly, but I'm going to use them. Just how, I don't know yet; but use them I shall."

And there they are in ornament V!

On another occasion, a friend of mine who was moving to the tropics asked me to give her a hand in toting a bunch of winter clothes to the hospital thrift shop. On a black velvet dress were two large rhinestone clips at the scooped-out neckline. "Hey, I'd sure like to have those clips. Could I?", I asked, feeling somewhat of a beggar.

"Gladly! But clips have been 'out' for years. They'd look really dowdy on you, my friend!"

"I'm not going to wear them."

"Well then, why do you want them?"

"I'm going to use them."

Her look was quizzical, but never mind. There they are: see "Kings of the Realm" III.

These are two of many instances where I came upon strange things which were put to use.

What are your favorite colors? You don't have to follow the crowd: You need not confine yourself to the proverbial, the classical red and green of Christmas. Try, instead, any color or color combinations that you're crazy about, and the result will be exciting. If the notion strikes you, go psychedelic: Combine hot pink and lime, brilliant orange and electric blue. You may want to experiment with rose, baby pink, yellow, sky blue, magenta, and of course the tried and true white. White for purity (I don't know that there are any virgins extant — but maybe), white for the driven snow, white for stealing a kiss under the mistletoe.

It may be that your idea is to have all the decorations the same color, say, all of them red or all green or all of them lime or pink. (I might add that this idea of narrowing your colors to one or two makes things easy, less challenging notwithstanding.) Now you can search out only the colors of "jewels" or buttons or braids or cording that will produce the picture you have in mind. Or, try matching colors or contrasting them on the same decoration. Often a very unlikely color can be used in conjunction with another, and you will find that the combination is effective: As in music, a dissonant passage will emphasize the grandeur of the whole. Experimenting is delightful.

eady? Go!

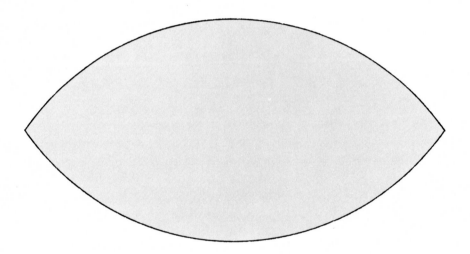

Above is the basic pattern used in cutting the fabric which is to cover the three-inch styrofoam ball.

Scale it up by about an inch all around for the larger ones (see Chapter "Kings of the Realm").

Scale it down (pattern below) for the tiny ones, such as those used for eardrops or for decorating candelabra.

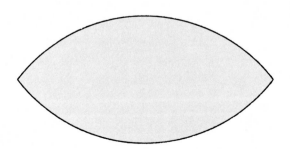

Begin by cutting the pattern from a piece of sturdy paper, such as a grocery bag. Pin it to your cloth. Cut a total of four of them, pin them, and cut out from cloth. With your small brush, put Elmer's glue on one of them and press it to the styrofoam ball. Rub it smooth and hold it until you're sure it has adhered. Do likewise on the opposite side, having the top and bottom ends barely touching.

You should have approximately the same amount of bare space on each of the two remaining uncovered sides. Now, cover these as you did the first two.

If there is any overlapping cloth, trim it away in order to have a nice smooth ball, even though you'll be covering the seams later by a braid, ribbon, etc. (Some materials are stretchy, some aren't at all. You will gauge this as you proceed.)

You may sometimes want to use two different colors on the same ball, or even four colors. Varying color combinations make for interest: For example, cover two opposite sides with lime green felt and the remaining two sides with, say, yellow or a rosy red or white.

Or, use a different color for each of the four quarters: cover north with bright pink, south with light pink, east with bright blue, west with light blue. Experiment with color combinations. Put your cloths side by side to see what looks harmonious or pleasingly contrasting.

Now take a look at the various ribbons, braids, weltings, cords, laces, sequins, metallic threads, beads, etc., and from them decide on your general design and colors. If you do not settle your scheme in advance, you may end up at sea: You will have, say, strung the beads on their wire, will have flanked them by the ribbon or cording you chose, only to find that you either don't have the right color braid or the right rope sequins to cover the four seams; or that, yes, you have the right color but not enough of it to go around!

Basic Technique

Step 1   Begin by making your center decoration in each of the four quarters. Start at the top of a quarter; center, let us say, a narrow ribbon at the top and bring it down to the center of the bottom of the quarter; take it up on the opposite quarter to the top where it will meet the end of the ribbon where you began. Cut the ribbon. Cut the same length for the two opposite quarters.

Step 2   Apply your glue on the "wrong side" of this center ribbon and apply the two lengths to the center of the four quarters. If you like the idea of "outlining" the ribbon with a contrasting cording or gold or silver metallic thread (or whatever you happen to have on hand), use a toothpick to make a very tiny line of glue on either side of the ribbon and apply your cording thus: Place two pins at the top of each quarter and two at the bottom on either side of the ribbon. Knot one end of the metallic thread around one of the top pins, bring the thread down and wind around the bottom pin. Continue outlining the ribbon, using the pins as anchors around which to wind the thread. Finally, insert the pins fully into the styrofoam.

Step 3   To cover the seams, you can use a wide braid, or a ribbon outlined by a band of sequins, or a welting outlined by a narrow metallic braid. Whichever you choose, measure how much you will need for half of the ball; cut two lengths of your seam-covering; or if you have chosen a combination of seam-covering materials, cut two lengths of each. Begin at the bottom. Glue on one half; then the other.

Step 4   Put a "finish" on the bottom, either a single large bead or a combination of beads. This latter choice will make a decorative "tail."

Step 5   With an ice pick, make two shallow holes (deep enough only to pierce through the braid or ribbon, etc.) in the center of the top of the finished ball; dip the ends of a hairpin in glue; insert the hairpin, leaving enough of it out for the hanger. If you do not intend to hang the ball but plan to use it in another manner, there is, of course, no need for the hairpin.

Some Stylish Models

Following are eighteen illustrations described in detail, along with a drawing of each ornament which diagrams the step-by-step execution of the decorating. Adopt or adapt some of these ideas if you wish; but you, yourself, may come up with some better ones of your own. The more decorations you make, the more innovations, the more inspirations!

Check out a few of the illustrations and you'll see how varied can be the styles: some are dainty, some dressy, others tailored. (For gifts to the occupants of a house or apartment which shows its owners have a penchant for bold colors, try using tweeds or wild plaids as a covering for the styrofoam.) You'll find examples of all these categories in the dozens of illustrations throughout the book.

The covering of the ball is red velvet.

Step 1   Begin, as always, by making the center decoration in each of the four quarters. Insert a pin through the green cording halfway into the ball at the top; bring the cording down to the center of the bottom; pin halfway; take it up the opposite quarter to the top of the ball. Cut the cording.

Now, do the same thing on the other two sides. (I suggest that you refer to Chapter "Helps" – Pins.) The reason for not inserting these pins fully is that you'll be using them later. (*Step 2.*)

Step 2   The green cording is "emphasized" by a silver metallic thread on each side of this green cording.

Make a slipknot in your metallic thread and put the knot on one of the top pins; take it down to the bottom pin and wind it once around this bottom pin to anchor it.

Go across to the opposite quarter and wind around; now up to the top; wind. Ditto for the two remaining sides. You will have no further use for these particular pins, so insert them fully now.

Step 3   Cover the seams of the four quarters with your ribbon. The one used in the illustration is white, with a silver Grecian key design embroidered.

Measure how much ribbon you will need to go once around the ball, leaving a smidgeon more for good measure. (It's easier to snip off than to add on!)

Cut two lengths of the ribbon.

Apply glue on the wrong side of one length.

Start at the bottom, take it up to the top, and down to the bottom.

Ditto procedure for the opposite remaining two seams.

Press the glued ribbon for a few minutes until you're sure it has adhered.

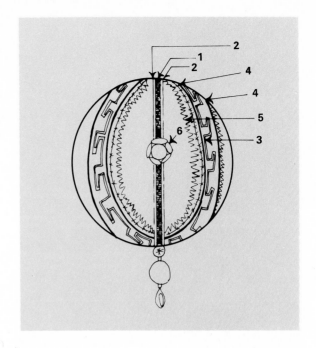

The green cording on both sides of the ribbon is applied in the same manner as was the center cording.

Step 4

Apply glue to the wrong side of this narrow silver braid and place it on the outer sides of the green cording. (Having measured how much is needed for one side, use this strip to cut three more.)

Step 5

The four center rhinestone decorations are buttons. Apply glue to the back of the button; secure it with two pins, the tips of which have been dipped in glue, and insert the pins in two of the tiny openings in the button. (If the holes of the button are large, put a sequin on the pin.)

Step 6

Bottom Decoration: Use a single large bead, or a combination such as is shown in the illustration. In the case that you don't wish to have a bottom decoration, you'll need several large sequins at the bottom to cover the ends of your trimmings.

On this ornament, there is a silver bead, a large white one, another small silver bead, a green crystal bead — all colors which have been used on the ball itself.

They have been put on a green-headed corsage pin; dip the tip of the pin in your little glue pot; insert.

With an ice pick, make two shallow holes (deep enough only to pierce through the ribbon) in the center of the top of the ball; dip the ends of the hairpin in glue; insert the hairpin, leaving enough of it free for the hanger. If you don't intend to hang the ball, but plan to use it in some other manner (filling a bowl, etc.) there is, of course, no need for the hairpin.

(See Chapter "Helps" — Hairpins and Glue.)

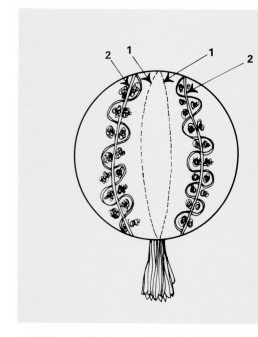

This one is a real glamour girl and yet very simple to make.

The covering is burnt gold felt for two opposite sides of the styrofoam ball; white felt for the other two.

Step 1   Insert halfway a pin at the top of each quarter and a pin at the bottom of each quarter. Measure how much of your fine wire is needed to go from the top to the bottom and back up to the top. Attach the wire to one of the top pins (see Chapter "Helps" – Pins); bead the wire, counting as you go along. (This counting will make it simpler when you bead the remaining seven lines.)

When you have beaded to the bottom, wind the wire once around the bottom pin and bead up to the top to form this pear shape.

Repeat the procedure in the remaining three quarters.

(If you don't find a very long wire awkward to handle, you could cut enough wire – plus a few inches extra – to bead two opposite quarters with the one wire. This would save a bit of time.

The silk and sequin braid is so handsome that there really is no necessity for a fancier central decoration than these two single lines of copper-colored beads. Don't you think that they suffice quite elegantly?

Step 2   The four seams are covered with a rich braid of light brown curlicue silk roping, intertwined with tan iridescent sequins. Piling on any more decoration on this ornament would be a bit of an overdose.

Measure off how much braid you will need to go once around the ball. Cut two lengths of the braid. Apply glue to the backside. Cover the four seams of the felt covering.

Bottom Decoration: This one is simply a "hank" of the copper-colored beads as they were purchased. This hank is secured by putting a bit of glue on the thread end of it and attaching it by two pins (on which have been put a gold sequin) dipped in glue.

Hairpin. (See Chapter "Helps" – Hairpins.)

24

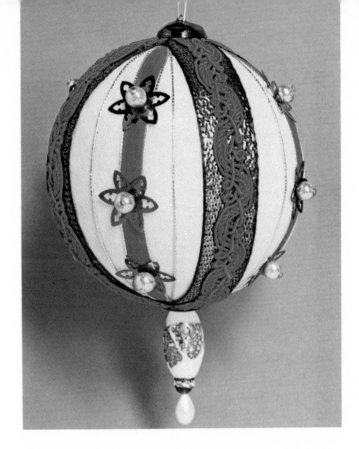

This one is very effective, yet simple and fast. It incorporates the traditional Christmas colors: red, green, silver, and white. The covering is white felt.

A narrow red velvet ribbon is glued down the center of each quarter. Measure and cut two lengths. Start at the top of the ball, go down and then up. Ditto for the opposite quarters. **Step 1**

Stick a pin, top and bottom of each quarter, on each side of the red ribbon — sixteen in all. **Step 2**

Make a slipknot in your silver metallic thread and outline both sides of the red velvet ribbon.

Using the same pins (top and bottom) as your means of anchoring, string the metallic silver thread in a pear-shape on both sides of the central red velvet, winding it once around the pins as you go along. **Step 3**

Measure off two lengths of the green tinselly Christmas ribbon. Glue. Apply over the seams. **Step 4**

The decorative red braid is superimposed on the green seam-covering ribbon. Glue backside. Apply. **Step 5**

The decoration on the red velvet ribbon is a silver "pearl" and a green "snowflake" sequin. Insert a pin through the two. Apply a touch of glue, and stick! I find that when you have a decoration of this sort (there are, of course, twelve of them), it's a time-saver to assemble all twelve (sequin and silver "pearl" on the pin) ahead of the time of applying them, rather than to assemble them one by one, piecemeal. (Stick them into a piece of cardboard or, better still, into a piece of styrofoam.) **Step 6**

Bottom Decoration: On a pearl-headed corsage pin are a long white bead (from an old necklace) on which there is red, green, and silver "glitter," a rondure of rhinestones, and a green crystal bead. Any substitutions, using the "incorporating" colors of the ornament, would be effective.

25

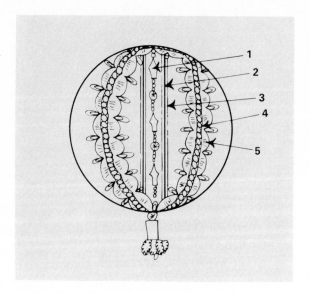

It's the combination of colors and textures which gives this one its oomph and interest: fuchsia, electric blue, bright yellow, gold.

The covering is fuchsia felt.

Step 1   Cut two lengths of wire sufficient to go around the ball (plus a few extra inches for good measure). Insert halfway a pin at top and at bottom (eight in all) of each quarter. Place slipknot over pin at the top. The beading here consists of a blue bugle bead, two little blue beads, a diamond-shaped yellow bead highlighted with gold, two little blue beads, an amber-colored rhinestone, repeat two little blue beads, repeat the diamond-shaped yellow one, repeat two little blue beads, repeat amber-colored rhinestone, repeat two little blue beads, repeat diamond-shaped yellow, finish to the bottom with a bugle bead. Wind wire once around bottom pin. Go across to bottom pin; wind wire once around.

Repeat the process on the two opposite quarters.

Step 2   On either side of the center beading is electric blue cording. Measure off enough to go twice around the ball. Cut two lengths of it. At the top, insert the pin halfway into the ball through the blue cording; bring to bottom; insert pin halfway. Repeat the process on the opposite quarter. This will, of course, bring you to the top. Now start down, over, and up to the top where you began.

Repeat the same cording procedure on the other side of the center decoration.

Do not insert the pins fully. You will be using them for the gold metallic thread.

Step 3   Outline the blue cording on both sides with gold metallic thread. Place slipknot over pin. Down, over, up; down, over, up, winding once around the pins as you come to them. Repeat on the other side of the cording. Repeat the metallic thread on both sides of the other blue cording.

Now insert fully all pins.

Step 4   A strand of single blue sequins covers the four seams.

Step 5   Bright yellow braid is placed on both sides of the blue sequins.

Bottom Decoration: The blue and the gold have been incorporated here, with a "canopy" (see "Make Your Own Thing" – Canopies) over the end of the corsage pin's head.

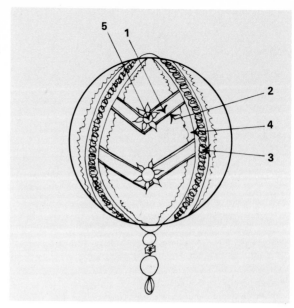

This one combines some really way-out colors: hot pink, bright orange, Kelly green, and gold. The covering is hot pink felt.

Step 1

Cut a length of the bright orange velvet narrow ribbon to a length adequate to fit half the "V" diagonal, i.e., from the seam of the quarter down to the middle of the quarter. Cut eight of these.

The ribbons for the lower "V" are a bit longer because the circumference of the ball there is greater. Cut eight of these.

In order that the "V's" be all at the same depth on the ball, measure from the top of each quarter. Stick a pin for your guide, or mark it with a pencil dot.

Glue on the four upper "V's."

Repeat the same process for the lower "V's."

Step 2

The outlining on both sides of the orange ribbon is green "straw" cording. With a toothpick, apply a bit of glue to the topside of the orange ribbon. Begin the Kelly green cording at the seam: Insert a pin halfway into the ball through the cording; take it to the center of the "V"; insert a pin fully. (It will be concealed later by the "pearl" and "snowflake" decoration.) Insert a pin halfway into the ball; wind the green cording once around; insert the pin fully.

Continue this process on the topside of the three remaining quarters; now, likewise for the bottom of the upper "V's."

Repeat the same process for the lower "V's."

Step 3

Apply the seam-covering. This one is a dressy upholstery braid (same orange as the velvet ribbon of the "V's").

Step 4

Bordering each side of the braid is a lacy Kelly green Christmas ribbon. Because it was originally more or less the same width as the orange braid, had I superimposed the braid upon this ribbon, it would have hardly been seen at all. So I cut it down the middle and applied it.

Step 5

A gold "pearl" and a large Kelly green "snowflake" sequin on a gold-headed pin (apply a bit of glue, of course, before inserting) are applied to the center of each of the eight "V's." They not only conceal the pins used to secure the Kelly green cording, but are quite a pretty touch, *n'est-ce pas?*

Bottom Decoration: Large beads incorporating the colors on the ornament.

VI

The covering is baby pink satin.

Because the central decorations (the rhinestone buttons) have no holes in them for pinning (see "Helps" – Center Decoration), place the four buttons where you'll be wanting to put them, mark off the space with pins, and make four holes with your ice pick and/or scissors barely large enough to accommodate the protrusion on the underside of the buttons.

The center beading is a combination of silver bugle beads and green beads.	**Step 1**
On each side of the center beading is bright green cording. Secure this cording with pins, top and bottom.	**Step 2**
The seam-covering is a bright green tinselly ribbon.	**Step 3**
On both sides of the ribbon is a narrow lacy braid.	**Step 4**
Apply glue to the bottom of the four buttons and insert.	**Step 5**

The bottom finish is a button almost identical to the ones on the ball except that it has an "emerald" in its center.

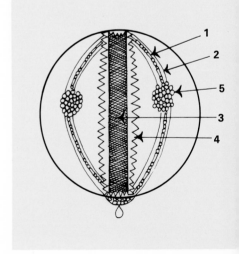

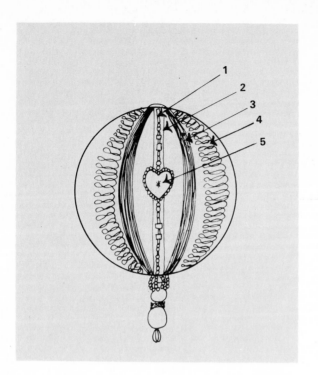

The covering of the ball is green satin.

Step 1   The center beading is of gold beads, tiny "pearls," and rhinestones, all of which are incorporated in the heart. (See "Helps" – Center Decoration.)

Step 2   Metallic gold thread outlines the central beading.

Step 3   Narrow red velvet ribbon is on both sides of the center, oval-shaped.

Step 4   A dainty gold braid is the seam-covering.

Step 5   Glue on the four hearts. The ones here came from a charm bracelet and therefore have a "loop" at the top. Apply glue to the hearts and to the pin, and place.

Bottom Decoration: A "canopy" of gold beads, a gold "pearl," a rondure of rhinestones, a large white "pearl," a gold-headed corsage pin.

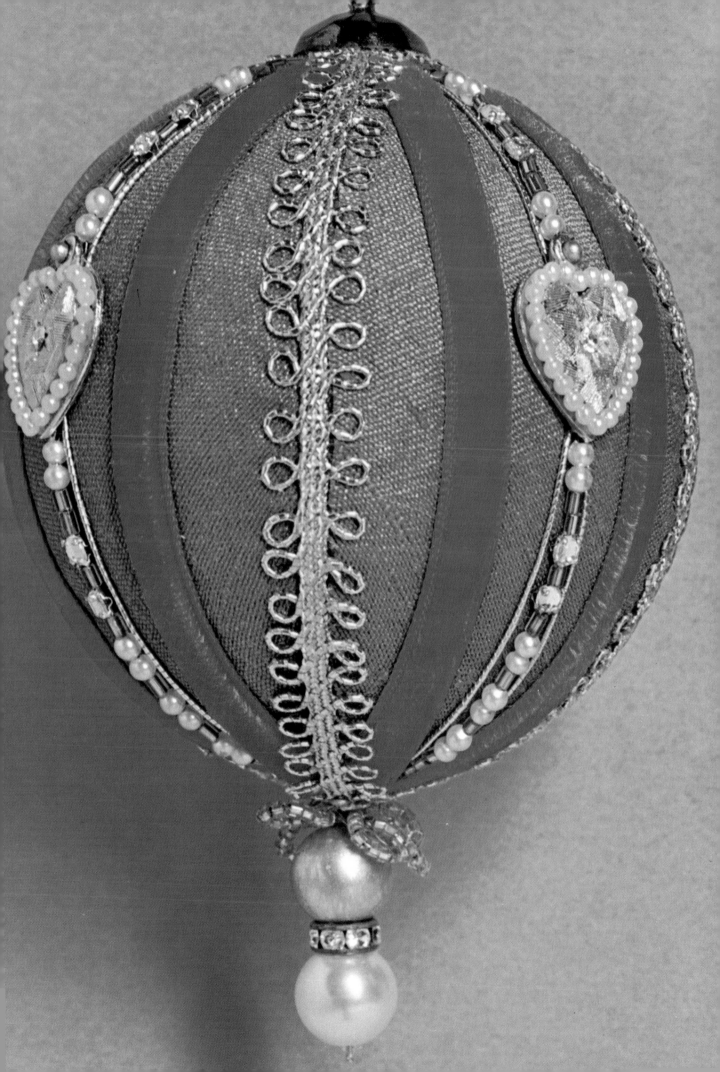

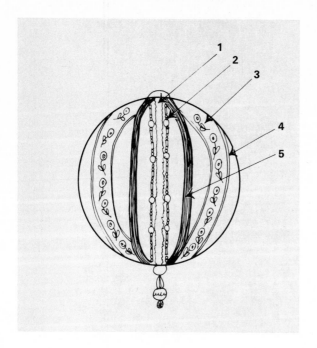

The covering is a loosely woven cerise wool.

Step 1   A tinselly narrow rose braid is in the center of each quarter.

Step 2   The beading on both sides of the narrow braid is composed of a green bugle bead, two tiny gold beads, a green bugle bead, two tiny gold beads, a hexagonal blue bead. Repeat to the bottom.

Step 3   The seam-covering is an old-fashioned bright blue ribbon embroidered with rose, pink, and cerise roses; green stem and leaves.

Step 4   The ribbon is outlined on both sides by gold metallic thread.

Step 5   A narrow green velvet ribbon outlines the center decoration.

The bottom decoration coordinates all the colors used on the ball: cerise, gold, blue (with a "canopy"), and green.

IX

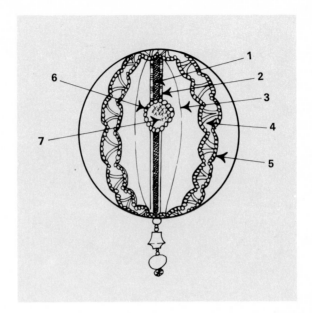

The covering is yellow felt.

In the center of each quarter is a chartreuse narrow braid, flecked with gold.

Step 1

The beading on both sides is a gold bugle bead, three copper-colored beads, repeat until you come to the top of where you will be putting the "frame." (See "Helps" – Center Decoration.) This "frame" is one of the ones referred to in the first paragraph of "Midas's Touch." Leaving adequate space for the center decoration, repeat the beading down to the bottom of the quarter.

Step 2

Gold metallic thread on both sides of the center decoration.

Step 3

Because of the openness of the braid, the seams of the yellow felt are covered with chartreuse grosgrain ribbon. (If not covered, they would show through the braid.)

Step 4

The braid is applied. It is a handsome one: copper-colored sequins, bronze metallic thread intertwined throughout.

Step 5

Apply glue to the back of the "frames" (I transformed these from black to copper-colored); apply glue to the back of the yellow crystal "diamond."

Steps 6 and 7

The bottom decoration repeats the tones of the ball: gold, bronze, copper.

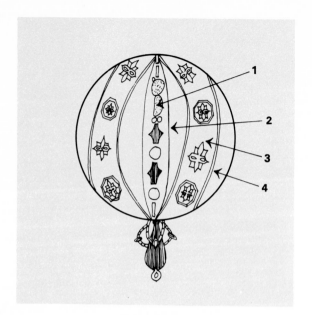

The covering is brilliant red velvet.

Step 1   The center beading consists of silver bugle beads, a link from a rhinestone bracelet, "pearls," two faceted crystal beads.

Step 2   The beading is outlined by silver metallic thread.

Step 3   The seam-covering is a handsome white ribbon embroidered in silver and red.

Step 4   The ribbon is edged with silver cording.

The bottom decoration has a "canopy" (see "Make Your Own Thing") of red bugle beads; the center of each loop has a faceted crystal bead. The silver "thing" came from an old hatpin! The head of the corsage pin is red.

XI

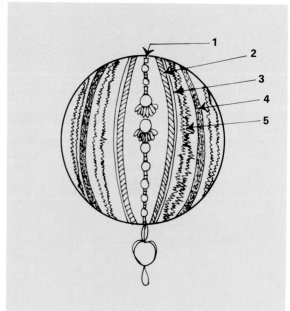

The covering is bright green mohair.

This decoration is included in the book to show (a) the effectiveness of various color combinations (green, gold, lavender, magenta, fuchsia, cerise, purple, and pink) and (b) the use to which unusual and large sequins can be put.

Step 1   Center beading. Between the larger beads whose colors are named above are gold bugle beads. The large shell-shaped gold sequins (with glue on the back, of course) are slipped beneath the cerise and the purple beads after the beading has been completed. These large sequins here give a lot of importance, don't they?

Step 2   Deep pink straw braiding on both sides of the beading.

Step 3   Gold metallic thread outlines the straw braiding.

Step 4   Lavender satin welting covers the seams.

Step 5   A lacy gold ribbon (which has been cut in half) is on both sides of the welting.

The bottom decoration consists of a large green sequin, a pear-shaped gold bead, a large cerise bead, gold corsage pin.

XII

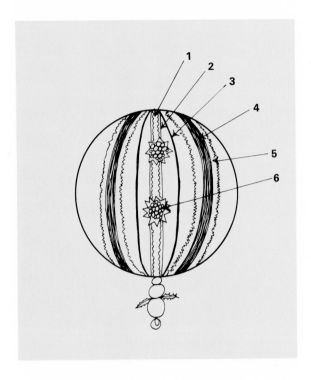

This decoration gives you a suggestion of the effectiveness of color combinations: forsythia yellow, green, pink, gold, purple, rose, blue.

The covering is yellow felt.

A rose-colored tinselly narrow braid is glued down the middle of each quarter. | Step 1

Gold metallic thread on each side of the braid. | Step 2

Bright green cording, to form an oval, on each side of the center strip. | Step 3

Purple welting over the seams. | Step 4

Narrow gold braid on both sides of the purple welting. | Step 5

Place on a gold-headed pin two rosettes of many-colored sequins (the colors in these rosettes are rose, blue, purple, pink, green, gold) and a large green "snowflake" sequin. | Step 6

The bottom decoration consists of: a rose-colored "pearl," a gold bead, a green "snowflake" sequin, a rosette of the many-colored sequins, a large purple bead — all on a rose-headed corsage pin.

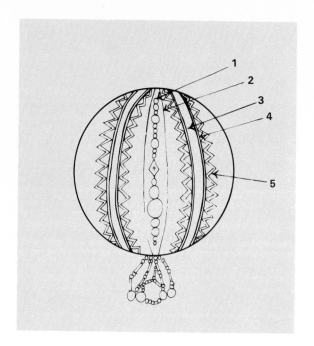

The covering is baby pink felt.

Step 1   The center decoration consists of two tiny seed "pearls" of pinkish cast, a rhinestone, another tiny seed "pearl," a hexagonal green flat bead, another tiny "pearl," another rhinestone, another tiny "pearl," a green bead, a "pearl," a diamond-shaped rhinestone (lines of pink and green in it), a lavender "pearl," a large-ish "pearl" of pinkish cast, a large lavender iridescent bead, and the line finishes with two "pearls" identical to the "pearl" above the lavender iridescent bead.

Step 2   Silver metallic thread on both sides of the beading.

Step 3   The seams are covered with lavender satin welting.

Step 4   Emerald green cording borders the lavender welting.

Step 5   Silver rickrack braid borders the green cording.
Bottom Decoration: This one shows how a "canopy" can be used for a stand-up ornament as well as one which you may wish to hang. (See Chapter "Sitting Ducks" and Chapter "Make Your Own Thing" – Canopies.) Each loop in this particular "canopy" is made thus: two of the tiny seed "pearls" of pinkish cast, then a silver bugle bead, two tiny seed "pearls," a green bugle bead, two tiny seed "pearls," a faceted green crystal bead. Repeat for other half of the loop of the "canopy."

Step 1	The covering is hot pink felt.
Step 2	A string of gold bugle beads in the center of each quarter.
	Cover the seams with narrow green velvet ribbon.
Step 3	The gold rickrack braid here is applied separately in each quarter. Measure the length from the top of one side of the velvet ribbon to the bottom. Cut eight of these. Glue, apply, secure top and bottom with gold-headed pins.
Step 4	The center decoration is a button: a green "crystal" surrounded by lacy gold. (See Chapter "Helps" — Center Decoration.)

Bottom Decoration: I didn't have what I considered an appropriate "jewel" for the bottom finish, so I concocted the one you see here. It is a long white bead on which I glued two lengths of the narrow green velvet ribbon and then glued on four lengths of the gold rickrack.

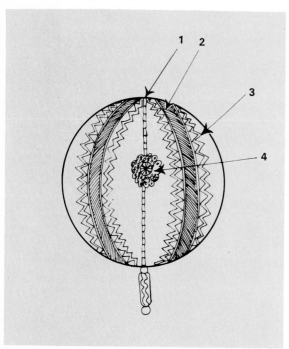

XV

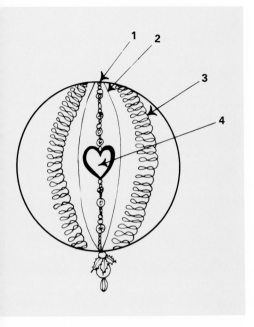

This is a sentimental one.

The covering is a delicate pink felt and would be appropriate for a little girl or for any female you love. You could choose blue or any color which strikes your fancy as a gift to a little boy or big male. (See VII, this chapter.)

The center beading is a combination of various sizes of "pearls" with a pinkish cast, tiny gold beads, and the gold heart. (Leave space for the heart. See Chapter "Helps" — Center Decoration.) I had only two of the gold hearts; so I used a pink crystal circle with a "pearl" stuck in its center for the other two quarters of the ornament.   **Step 1**

Gold metallic thread is on the sides of the center beading.   **Step 2**

A dainty gold braid covers the four seams of the pink felt covering.   **Step 3**

Glue is applied on the backside of the two hearts.   **Step 4**

The bottom decoration is a gold "pearl," a "canopy" of tiny gold beads over a large pink "pearl," all on a pink-headed corsage pin. (See Chapter "Make Your Own Thing" — Canopies.)

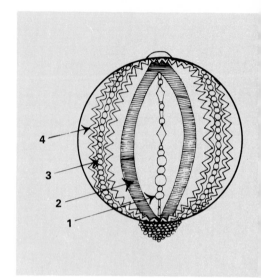

This ornament is included in the book for two reasons: (a) Because the covering is wool mohair, the seams do not show and therefore it lent itself to being a three-sided ornament. And (b) because one lone eardrop can be put to good use. (I, myself, think that the only thing worse than losing *two* eardrops is losing *one* eardrop.) Here, the single eardrop is used as the bottom decoration. It was pried loose from its holder, and secured to the ball by two gold-headed pins.

(See Chapter "Be Two-Faced" — Three-Faced.)

Step 1   Make three strings of beading at equidistant points. Here, there is a combination of tiny gold "pearls," gold bugle beads, larger gold "pearls," two large shiny blue "pearls," and two diamond-shaped blue beads flecked with gold.

Step 2   Apply the light blue narrow velvet ribbon in a pear-shape on both sides of the beading.

Step 3   Apply the strand of brilliant blue sequins between (in the middle of) the two bands of velvet ribbon.

Step 4   Apply the rickrack to both sides of the strand of sequins.

XVII

This ornament is included in the book to show what you can do when you have only two ornaments, yet four quarters to decorate. (These two were earrings.) Covering is cerise wool.

The center line is narrow avocado green straw braid. — **Step 1**

On both sides of it is strung a line of gold bugle beads. — **Step 2**

Beyond the bugle beads, yellow silk cording. — **Step 3**

Apply the narrow avocado green velvet ribbon. — **Step 4**

Secure the two center ornaments by glue on the backside and three gold "pearls" on a gold-headed pin dipped in glue. These "pearls" are security as well as an added embellishment. On the two sides without the center ornamentation, the braid, the bugle beads, and the yellow silk cording are quite enough decoration indeed! — **Step 5**

Note that all the colors of the center decoration have been incorporated in the rest of this ornament: cerise flower — cerise woolen covering; green leaves — green straw braid and green velvet ribbon; yellow flowers — yellow silk cording; gold "pearls" — gold bugle beads; white flowers — white "pearls" on the bottom decoration.

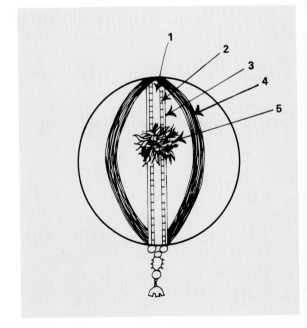

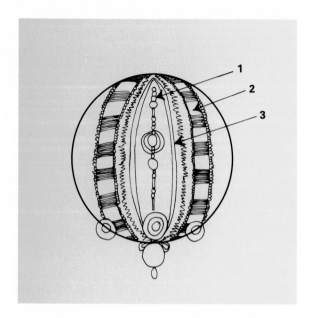

This decoration is included in the collection of this book to show a different type of bottom decoration: At the bottom of each string of beading, there is a large pink "pearl" set in a pink crystal circle. Ditto for the center of the bottom.

Step 1   A silver bugle bead, three tiny pink "pearls," a silver "pearl," a pink "pearl," a silver bugle bead, three tiny pink "pearls," a large pink "pearl" set in a pink crystal circle, a tiny pink "pearl," a large one, two tiny pink "pearls," a silver bugle bead make up the center string of beading.

Step 2   A pink ribbon on which is intertwined silver metallic thread is the seam-covering.

Step 3   A lacy silver Christmas ribbon which has been cut in half (see Chapter "Helps") outlines both sides of the center beading.

The eight decorations illustrated in this chapter show what can be achieved by beading only two quarters instead of the four, all the while obtaining with less exertion and less time a really dramatic result.

The first three of them have two opposite quarters covered with a cocktail-dress cloth of white satin embroidered in gold, which cloth is so decorative in itself that there is no need to dress it up further. The opposite two quarters are covered in felt: red, blue, pink. The fourth in this series is covered entirely in this same gold-embroidered cloth, with but two of the quarters beaded.

The last four decorations show two of the quarters covered in a "loud" green and blue basket-weave woolen plaid. The opposite two quarters (on which is the beading) are of felt: the blue or the green of the plaid.

If you have an interesting printed cloth, use this print for two of the quarters. For covering the remaining two quarters, select a cloth which matches one of the colors of the print; or use two different colors of the plain cloth which pick up two of the colors of the print.

When you find that a cloth doesn't show seams, try making a *three-faced* ornament. Wool mohair, nubby wools, many loosely woven materials as well as lacy, open cloths will serve this purpose. You must watch, however, that all the three sections are of equal dimension, i.e., equidistant from each other, and that the bottom point is directly beneath the top point: Begin at the center of the top and at the center of the bottom of the ball. If not, your bottom decoration will be off-center. Mark these top and bottom points with a corsage pin — to be removed, of course, after you have determined where your three lines of trimming are to be placed.

Begin by pinning a narrow ribbon or braid at the three equidistant points; check to see that all three thirds are equal and that the top and bottom are in line. This is a trial run. Mark off with pins where these three lines are to be when you begin your decorating plan.

You will be glad to know how to make these three-faced numbers when, for instance, you have only three of a "jewel" or only enough braid or ribbon for three lines instead of the customary four.

Examples of the *three-faced* ornaments are found in the following chapters: "Sitting Ducks" III and V; "Kings of the Realm" I and II, and "Some Stylish Models" XVI.

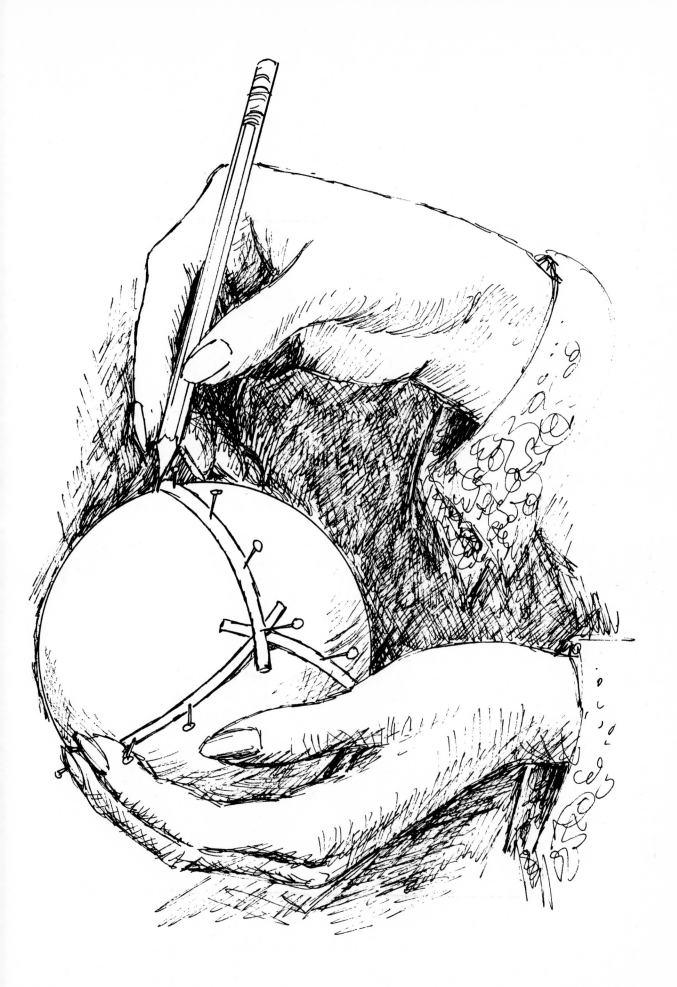

The covering: Two quarters are of white satin embroidered in gold; the two beaded quarters are of baby pink felt.

Step 1   The circles of pink crystal beneath the two central lavender "pearls" are glued onto the felt. Allow to dry a few minutes. Now the center beading: faceted rose crystal beads of varying sizes and shapes, faceted lavender crystal, lavender "pearls," tiny gold beads, and gold "pearls."

Step 2   This center beading is outlined by a purple cording.

Step 3   On the outer side of the purple cording, gold metallic thread.

Step 4   Cover the seams with a decorative gold braid.
Bottom Decoration: A large baroque rose "pearl," a gold "pearl," a rose-headed corsage pin.

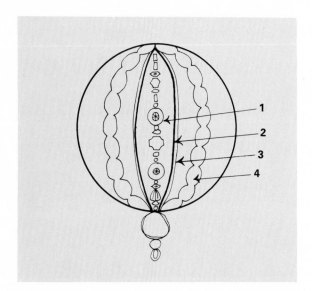

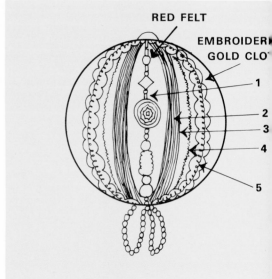

RED FELT

EMBROIDER
GOLD CLO

1
2
3
4
5

The covering: Two quarters are of white satin embroidered in gold; the two beaded quarters are of fire-engine red.

Step 1   The beading consists of varying shapes and textures and sizes of green and gold beads. Before securing the wire of the beading at the bottom of the ball, ascertain that you have left enough space to place the gold circle around the faceted green crystal.

Step 2   Beside the center beading are two strips of narrow green straw braid.

Step 3   On both sides of the straw braid is a gold metallic thread.

Step 4   The lacy gold Christmas ribbon (which has been cut down the center) is applied.

Step 5   Braid, green flecked with gold, is applied over the seams.

Bottom Decoration: A piece of gold necklace. Secure it by gold-headed pins.

The covering: two quarters are of white satin embroidered in gold; the two beaded quarters are of sky blue felt.

Glue on the little gold frame. The beads are of all shapes, textures, sizes, and colors: chartreuse, lavender, pink, gold, and green. **Step 1**

A double row of yellow silk cording outlines this center beading. **Step 2**

A yellow and gold braid covers the seams. **Step 3**

Bottom Decoration: A large baroque pink "pearl" is embellished by a six-sided "canopy" of little gold beads; the head of the corsage pin is lavender. (For instructions on making the "canopy," see Chapter "Make Your Own Thing" — Canopies.)

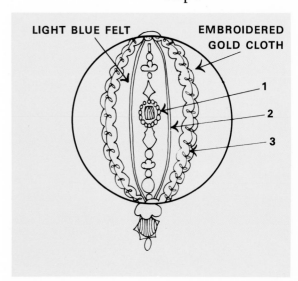

LIGHT BLUE FELT   EMBROIDERED GOLD CLOTH

1

2

3

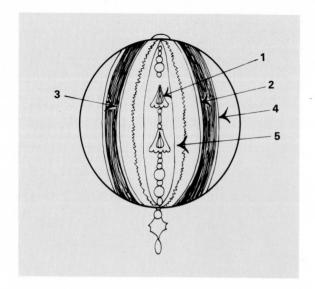

All four quarters are covered in the white satin embroidered in gold.

Step 1   The center beading is made up of varying shapes and sizes and colors: gold, blue, cerise, purple. After the beading is completed, apply a bit of glue on the backs of the two large "shell" sequins and slip carefully beneath two of the "jewels."

Step 2   Two of the seams are covered with narrow rose velvet ribbon.

Step 3   The other two seams are covered with narrow lavender velvet ribbon.

Step 4   On both sides of the velvet ribbons is applied turquoise blue cording.

Step 5   Measure how much narrow gold braid you will need for half of the oval which surrounds the center beading. Glue; apply; secure, top and bottom, with a gold sequin pin.

Bottom Decoration: A cerise "pearl," an irregularly shaped purple bead, a lavender corsage pin.

Two of the quarters are covered in green felt; the other two opposite in a "loud" green and blue basket-weave woolen plaid.

Step 1   The center beading is made up of silver and green beads. (See Chapter "Helps" — Center Decoration.) Verify the amount of room you leave to accommodate this handsome silver and green and rhinestone button. It is applied later in *Step 5*.

Step 2   Silver cording on both sides of the center beading.

Step 3   Narrow Kelly green velvet ribbon is applied over the seams.

Step 4   A narrow, dressy silver braid borders the velvet ribbon.

Step 5   Apply the button.

Bottom Decoration: A twisted rope of silver beads, a faceted green crystal bead, a silver-headed corsage pin.

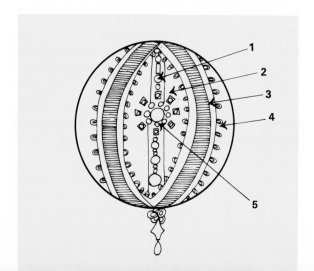

VI

Two of the quarters are covered in blue felt; the opposite two in a "loud" green and blue basket-weave woolen plaid.

Center beading: silver "pearls" of varying sizes, silver bugle beads, faceted crystal beads. Before securing wire at bottom of the ball, verify the space for the rhinestone pin. (See Chapter "Helps" — Center Decoration.) **Step 1**

A narrow white and silver braid borders the line of beading. **Step 2**

A lacy silver braid covers the seams. **Step 3**

Apply the rhinestone pin: Glue backside, pins here and there. **Step 4**

Bottom Decoration: A large Kelly green sequin, a large silver "pearl," a faceted crystal bead, a blue crystal bead, a silver-headed corsage pin.

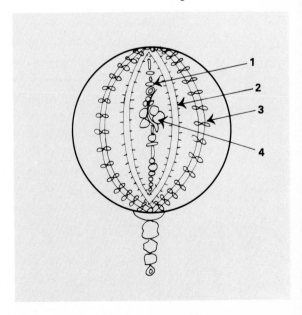

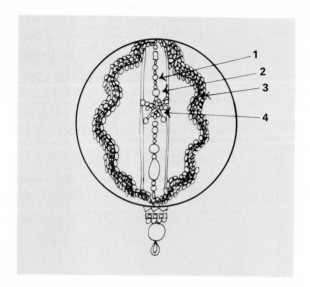

Two of the quarters are covered in blue felt; the opposite two in a "loud" green and blue basket-weave woolen plaid.

Step 1   Center beading: silver "pearls" of varying sizes, white beads, green crystal beads. Before securing the wire at the bottom of the ball, verify the space for the decoration in the center of the line of beading. (See Chapter "Helps" — Center Decoration.) This decoration is to be applied later in *Step 4*.

Step 2   A very narrow silver ribbon borders the line of beading.

Step 3   A handsome curlicue braid of white intertwined by a band of silver sequins is applied over the seams.

Step 4   Secure the center decoration (a link of a necklace) by gluing backside, pins here and there.

Bottom Decoration: A silver bead, a rondure of rhinestones, another silver bead like the first, a large silver "pearl," a green-headed corsage pin.

Two of the quarters are covered in green felt; the opposite two in a "loud" green and blue basket-weave woolen plaid.

Step 1   The center beading is made up of varying shapes and sizes of faceted crystal beads, green beads, silver "pearls." The center rhinestone decoration will be applied later in *Step 4.* (See Chapter "Helps" — Center Decoration.)

Step 2   A narrow white, curvy braid touched with silver borders the line of beading.

Step 3   Silver roping covers the seams.

Step 4   Apply the center decoration. Glue backside, pin here and there.

Bottom Decoration: A silver "pearl," a faceted crystal bead, a faceted "emerald," a silver-headed corsage pin.

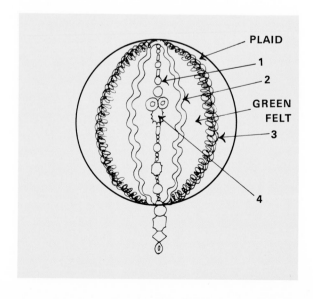

ithout Benefit of Bangles

You can make some outstanding decorations by concentrating on design and color combinations, minus "jewels."

Have a look at numbers I, II, and III. All three use almost the very same materials, yet give an entirely different effect. The materials are: a red and yellow basket-weave upholstery material for the covering, a narrow red horsehair braid, a silky red passementerie on I and II, a red cotton curlicue braid on III, and a yellow thread which was unravelled from the same red and yellow upholstery material with which all three decorations are covered.

Step 1   Glue two strips of the narrow red horsehair braid, barely wide enough apart to accommodate the silky passementerie, over the four seams. Now glue two more strips of this same horsehair braid equidistant from your first two strips; again, ditto for the two remaining quarters. This will give you four complete strips. (You could make the usual two seam-coverings, but I think that the four make a more attractive decoration.)

Step 2   Apply the yellow thread on the outer edges of the red horsehair.

Step 3   Apply the passementerie.

The bottom decoration is simply a faceted red bead; gold corsage pin.

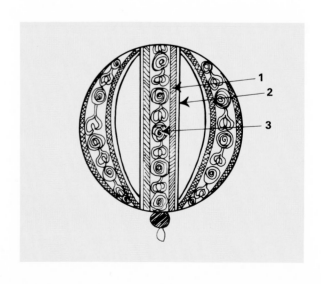

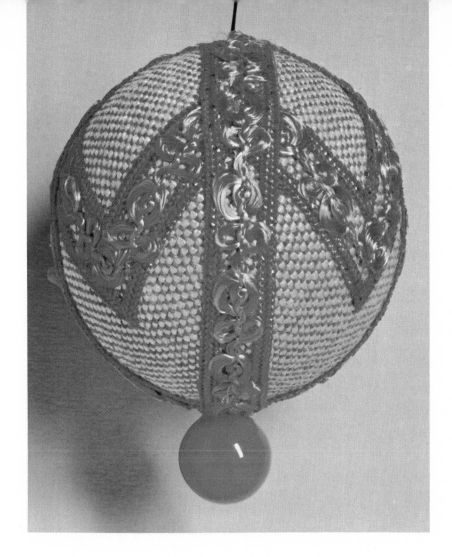

Same covering as on I; same narrow red horsehair braid; same red passementerie.

For the "V" in the four quarters, measure from the seam down to the top of the middle of the "V." Cut eight of these lengths of the narrow red horsehair braid.

Step 1

Cut eight lengths for the bottom of the "V." (These latter will be a tiny bit longer than the top ones.)

Glue this red horsehair braid to one quarter.

Mark with a pin where the next "V" is to go so that all the "V's" will be at the same depth.

Ditto for the remaining two "V's."

Glue on the red passementerie between the two strips of narrow red horsehair braid.

Step 2

Now, apply the horsehair braid on each side of the four seams.

Step 3

Glue on the passementerie.

Step 4

Bottom Decoration: One big red bead.

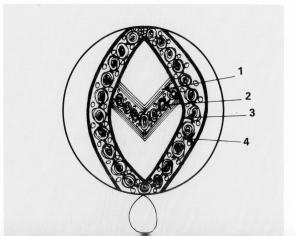

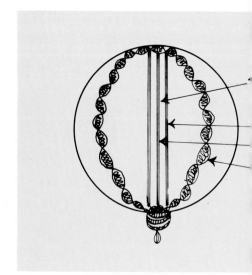

Same covering, same narrow red horsehair braid, same yellow thread. Only the braid which covers the seams is different.

Step 1   Glue on two strips of the horsehair braid in the center of each quarter, just wide enough apart to accommodate the yellow thread.

Step 2   Yellow thread on the outer sides of the horsehair braid.

Step 3   Yellow thread between the two strips of horsehair braid.

Step 4   Red cotton curlicue braid covers the four seams.

Bottom Decoration: A faceted red bead; gold-headed corsage pin.

IV

The covering is an avocado green basket-weave wool.

Apply the gold horsehair narrow braid on each side of the four seams, barely wide enough apart to accommodate the red passementerie.   **Step 1**

A yellow silk cording on the outer sides of the gold horsehair braid.   **Step 2**

Glue on the red passementerie.   **Step 3**

Begin at the bottom of the ball and glue on the red rope welting.   **Step 4**

Bottom Decoration: A large gold sequin to cover the raw ends of the welting. Then a large amber bead; gold-headed corsage pin.

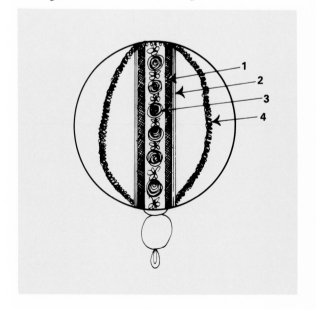

V

This number is very simple to make, yet very attractive because of the colors and the combinations of textures.

The covering is lime green felt.

Step 1   Glue a single strand of silver sequins down the middle of each quarter.

Step 2   Apply the blue braid over the four seams.

Step 3   A lacy narrow silver braid borders each side of the blue braid.

Bottom Decoration: A silver baroque "pearl," a large blue bead, another silver baroque "pearl," a lime green corsage pin.

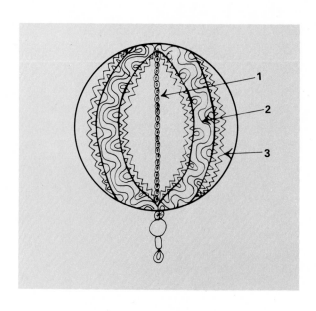

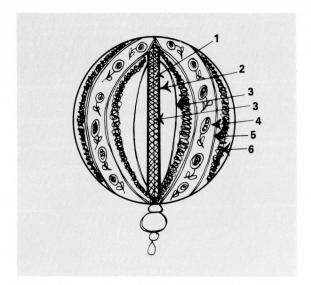

VI

The covering is lime green felt.

Step 1   Glue a narrow, tinselly rose braid down the center of each quarter.

Step 2   A cerise cording is on each side of it.

Step 3   A silver metallic thread is just beyond the cerise cording as well as down the middle of the tinselly rose braid.

Step 4   This charming blue ribbon embroidered with roses of pink, rose, and cerise and green stem and leaves is applied over the four seams.

Step 5   A Kelly green cording is on both sides of the embroidered ribbon.

Step 6   A lacy silver Christmas ribbon borders the green cording.

Bottom Decoration: A cerise "pearl," a large iridescent blue bead, a magenta "pearl," blue corsage pin.

VII

Lime green felt is the covering.

Measure the distance from the seam to the bottom of the top "V." Cut eight of these lengths of rose cording. Ditto for the bottom "V." (These bottom ones will be a "twee" longer.) Mark with pins (or a pencil dot) where the bottoms of the eight "V's" are to be placed so that their placing is uniform. Glue on the cording in the four quarters.   **Step 1**

Insert pins halfway into the styrofoam at the seam, top and bottom of the rose cording, as well as top and bottom of the center of the "V." You will need these pins (wind once around, a bit of glue applied, and insert fully) as you border the rose cording with gold metallic thread.   **Step 2**

The seams are covered with blue welting.   **Step 3**

Gold metallic thread on both sides of the blue welting.   **Step 4**

Rose cording just beyond the gold thread.   **Step 5**

A narrow, dainty deep yellow braid borders the rose cording.   **Step 6**

An iridescent button (glue backside and gold-headed pin) decorates the eight "V's."   **Step 7**

Bottom Decoration: A gold bead, a rose "pearl," a gold-headed corsage pin.

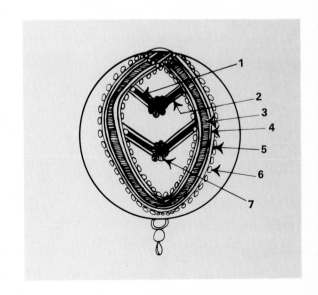

VIII

This number is covered in four different colors of felt: a light periwinkle blue, a light turquoise blue opposite; a lime green, a Christmas green opposite.

Step 1   Measure the length from seam to seam of the quarter. Cut four lengths of these from the sky blue straw braid. Ditto for the bottom strip of straw braid. Mark with a pin or pencil dot (these will not be seen because of the seam-covering later) so that they will be all at the same height on the ball. (Otherwise, they won't be "meeting" each other in an unbroken line!) Glue the straw braid now.

Step 2   Insert pins halfway into the styrofoam on the top and the bottom of the straw braid at the seam. You will use these to "anchor" the gold metallic thread: Wind it once around the pin, apply a bit of glue, insert pin fully.

Step 3   The same straw braid covers the four seams.

Step 4   A purple cording borders the braid.

Step 5   A dainty baby blue braid borders the purple cording.

Bottom Decoration: A large green sequin to conceal any raw ends; an oval green bead; a green corsage pin.

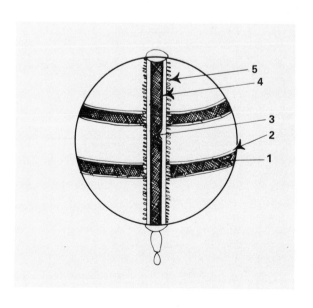

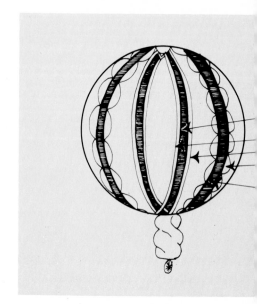

The covering is brilliant pumpkin-colored basket-weave wool.

Step 1   Measure the blue horsehair braid to a length adequate to make an oval in the center of each quarter. Cut eight lengths of it.

Step 2   With your tiny brush or a toothpick, apply glue (one side at the time so that the glue doesn't dry before you apply the cording) to the inner sides of the blue horsehair braid; now, apply the forsythia yellow cording. The outer sides of the horsehair braid are bordered by magenta silk cording.

Step 3   Magenta woolen braid is applied over the four seams of the covering.

Step 4   The narrow blue horsehair braid is applied in the center of the magenta wool braid.

Bottom Decoration: A large irregularly shaped blue bead on a gold corsage pin.

X

The same bright pumpkin-colored wool as the foregoing covers the ball.

With this bright turquoise blue straw braid, measure the distance between the seams a length adequate to form these "X's." (Be a wee bit generous: you can always cut off a smidgeon if too long.) Mark with a pin or pen or pencil dot (the seam-covering will cover the marking) so that they all start at the same height at the top and at the same depth at the bottom. Glue on.

Step 1

With your tiny brush or a toothpick, to one side of the blue straw braid; apply the cerise cording. Ditto for opposite side. Now, apply the cording in the same manner to the other line of the "X." Go to the next quarter, and to the third, and to the fourth after checking your markings.

Step 2

A cerise silk welting covers the seams.

Step 3

A dainty baby blue braid borders the cerise welting.

Step 4

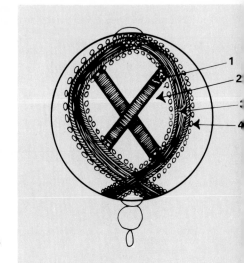

Bottom Decoration: A large sequin to cover any raw ends, a large blue bead, a gold corsage pin.

You can see from these "without benefit of bangles" (and the same principle can be applied to any category of these decorations) that you can make dozens of balls with the same color of covering, but with varying designs and varying trimmings and, yet, no two of them have the slightest resemblance one to the other. For example, I had an order for two dozen shocking pink ones. They were all shocking pink all right, but it ended there. Each was "individualized" because of the differing concepts of design as well as the differing ribbons and braids and cordings on each ball. Each, therefore, had its own cachet: pink and lavender, pink and red, pink and blue, pink and lime, pink and white, pink and green, and pink and you-name-it!

And now that I think of it, I can tell you that I have never made any two alike. What a bore that would be!

Sitting Ducks

These ornaments that "sit" have many a use. How festive they are on a mantel, on the shelves of a hutch, on a desk top, on bookcases, on secretaries (the furniture kind!), on the lowboy in your foyer, in front of each guest as a place card. You may want to have one of the very large ones (see Chapter "Kings of the Realm") as the centerpiece to grace your Christmas dinner table. If you choose to "sit" it atop a base, see the decorated bases of the trees in the Chapter "Tannenbaum," as well as the base for the candelabrum. (See Chapter "Other Ways, Other Uses" — Candelabra, Candlesticks, Miniature Trees.)

I, myself, have used them not only as place cards during the Christmas season, but at Thanksgiving as well. And because "Christmas is just around the corner," the guests were delighted at receiving them. As place cards, there are several ways in which you can designate the name of the recipient: One is to stand a little folding place card (found in any stationery store) in front of them; another is to make a card (a very tiny one so as not to hide any of the ornament's decoration), punch a small hole in the corner, string a length of metallic thread through, knot, and tie in a bow through the hairpin: "To Ann. Christmas ____. Connie." (See Chapter "Helps" — Cards.) This use as a place card is very gay on a table, as well as flattering to family or guests because of its being personalized, individualized.

As to the various means of having these ornaments "sit," there are several methods. (See Chapter "Make Your Own Thing" — Rings and Canopies.) Another is simply to put several large beads on a corsage pin and insert, slantwise, at four equidistant points. (See VI, this chapter.)

The covering is a rosy red, loosely woven wool.

Step 1   The center beading consists of varying sizes of gold "pearls," gold bugle beads, and faceted amber crystal beads.

Step 2   This beading is outlined by yellow silk cording.

Step 3   The gold braid is applied over the seams.

Secure the ring of large gold "pearls" on the bottom (see Chapter "Make Your Own Thing" — Rings) and secure an ornamentation at the top (here it is of gold "pearls" which was, until it was pried from its holder, an eardrop.) Simply glue backside and pin.

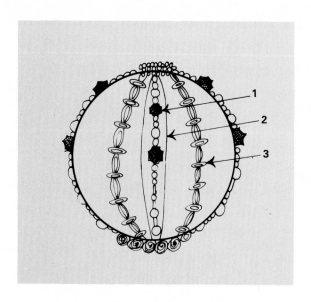

The covering is baby pink felt.

Step 1   The center beading consists of pink "pearls," rhinestones, a lavender "pearl," a silver "pearl," a purple "pearl."

Step 2   A silver metallic thread borders this center beading.

Step 3   A narrow rose velvet ribbon covers two of the seams; a lavender one, the other two.

Step 4   A purple cording on both sides of the velvet ribbons.

Step 5   A dainty, open-work braid is applied beyond the purple cording.

Bottom Decoration (See Chapter "Make Your Own Thing" — Canopies): This "canopy" has four loops. Each loop has two tiny pink "pearls," a silver bugle bead, two tiny pink "pearls," a purple bugle bead, two tiny pink "pearls," a lavender "pearl," two tiny pink "pearls," a rose bugle bead, two tiny pink "pearls," a silver bugle bead, two tiny pink "pearls."

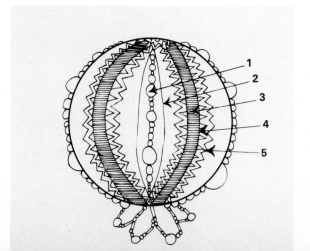

III

The covering is Kelly green woolen mohair. Because mohair doesn't show seams, this ornament is three-sided instead of the usual four.

The center beading is at three equidistant points and consists of a line of green and silver bugle beads. (Leave space for the center ornamentation, *Step 5*. See Chapter "Helps" — Center Decoration.)

Step 1

Silver cording borders this line of beading.

Step 2

A narrow white braid flecked with silver is applied at equidistant points, i.e., between the line of beading.

Step 3

A narrow pumpkin-colored velvet ribbon is applied in an oval shape, bordering the white and silver braid.

Step 4

The ring on the bottom (see Chapter "Make Your Own Thing" — Rings) is made of two "pearls," one large silver "pearl"; repeat three more times.

The top decoration is a very large faceted sequin secured by six pins (at equidistant points) on which have been put two small "pearls." Put a "twee" of glue on the sequin where the "pearls" are to touch it.

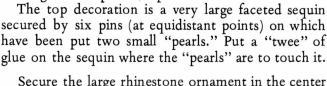

Secure the large rhinestone ornament in the center of the line of beading: glue on backside, put a silver "pearl" on a pin, insert two of these in the two top openings of the ornament.

Step 5

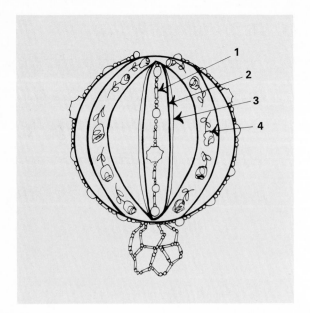

The covering is hot pink felt.

Step 1   The center beading consists of two tiny gold beads, a blue crystal bead, two tiny gold beads, a gold bugle bead, two tiny gold beads, a flat green crystal bead, two tiny gold beads, a gold bugle bead, two tiny gold beads, a faceted blue bead, two tiny gold beads, a gold bugle bead, two tiny gold beads, the flat green crystal bead, two tiny gold beads, a gold bugle bead, two tiny gold beads, the blue crystal bead, two tiny gold beads, a gold bugle bead, two tiny gold beads.

Step 2   A blue cording borders this beading.

Step 3   Gold metallic thread on the outer side of the blue cording.

Step 4   A blue ribbon embroidered with roses of pink, rose, and hot pink, and green stem and leaves is applied over the seams.

The bottom decoration is two "canopies," one of green bugle beads and tiny gold beads, and one of blue bugle beads and tiny gold beads. (See Chapter "Make Your Own Thing" — Canopies.) These are secured by a pink-headed corsage pin.

The covering is nubby white upholstery material which doesn't show seams. Therefore this is a three-sided ornament.

The center is made up of faceted lavender crystal beads, lavender "pearls," gold "pearls," gold bugle beads, and a large lavender crystal (flecked with gold) bead with gold metal "canopies" on the top and bottom of it. (You find these very often on costume jewelry and they're very useful because they give a lot of importance to a "jewel.") **Step 1**

Purple cording on both sides of the center beading. **Step 2**

Gold metallic thread on outer sides of cording. **Step 3**

Narrow lavender velvet ribbon at the three equidistant points between the three lines of beading. **Step 4**

The gold braid would have been too wide to use as is, and too narrow to allow the velvet ribbon to be superimposed on it; so it is cut down the center and applied on both sides of the lavender velvet ribbon. (Before you cut it, apply glue on the backside; otherwise it will fray. See Chapter "Helps.") **Step 5**

The bottom decoration is a ring (see Chapter "Make Your Own Thing" — Rings) of gold "pearls": a large one, a smaller one, etc., until you have the circumference you judge appropriate.

The top decoration is an eardrop made up of faceted lavender crystal beads and lavender "pearls." At its base is gold filigree. Secure by means of gold-headed pins through the filigree.

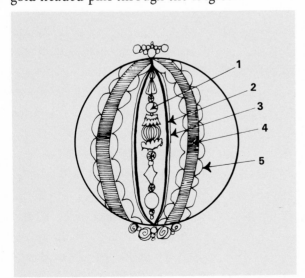

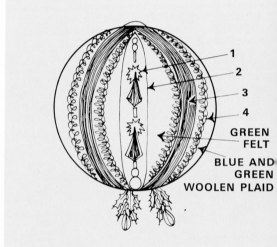

This is a two-faced ornament. Two of the quarters are a "loud" blue and green basket-weave wool; the opposite two are of green felt.

Step 1   The center beading is: a silver bugle bead, a tiny silver "pearl," a flat blue bead, a tiny silver "pearl," a silver bugle bead; allow space for the faceted blue pendant which is secured by a blue-headed pin into a fancy silver sequin; another silver bugle bead; repeat, after allowing space for the blue pendant, the beading with a silver bugle bead, a blue "pearl," a crystal bead, a silver "pearl."

Step 2   Silver cording borders the center beading.

Step 3   A narrow Kelly green velvet ribbon covers the four seams.

Step 4   A lacy Christmas ribbon borders both sides of the velvet ribbon.

The bottom decoration is a large silver bead, an irregularly-shaped blue "pearl" on a silver-headed corsage pin. Insert the pins slantwise so that the ball will stand straight. (See last paragraph of the introduction of this chapter.)

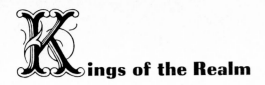

Kings of the Realm

These are six-inch styrofoam balls. At first glance, they look forbidding, but *au contraire*. Use exactly the same techniques you've used on the smaller sizes. These large ones are very impressive indeed and also have the advantage of giving you the opportunity of using some of the very large "jewels" you have in your storehouse of treasures, too large for the smaller sizes.

On these very large balls, use a large-sized hairpin at the top for the hanger. (See Chapter "Helps" — Hairpins.) When you hang them on your Christmas tree, place them on the bottom branches. Otherwise, your tree will look topheavy.

Use the same pattern for cutting your covering as for the other balls, but enlarge the quarters by an inch to an inch and a half all around. As you've found out, the size of the quarters depend on the stretchiness of the cloth.

Select large braids and ribbons and "jewels" so that your finished decoration won't have a "dinky" look.

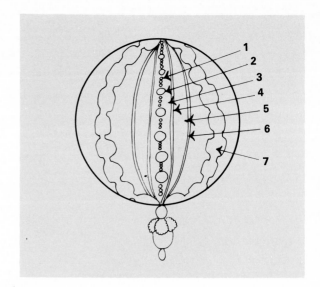

The covering: first cover the ball with rose satin; then with gold-embroidered white lace.

Because the covering is the eye-catching feature of this decoration, I didn't want to conceal it with too much added decoration; so I chose to make it a three-sided one.

Step 1 A narrow pink straw braid is applied at three equidistant points. This braid is barely seen. Its sole purpose is to act as a guide, nothing more.

Step 2 The beading simply consists (so as not to detract from the covering) of tiny gold beads between a succession of pink "pearls" and gold "pearls."

Step 3 Apply a yellow silk cording on both sides of the beading.

Step 4 Gold metallic thread is on the outer side of the cording.

Step 5 A bit beyond (about three-fourths inch at the middle), the yellow silk cording is repeated.

Step 6 Again, the gold metallic thread on the outer side of the yellow cording.

Step 7 A gold braid at the three equidistant points.

Bottom Decoration: An iridescent rose "pearl"; a "canopy" (see Chapter "Make Your Own Thing" — Canopies) of gold beads; a very large pink baroque "pearl"; a gold-headed corsage pin.

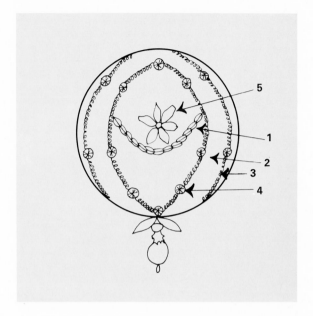

This is another three-sided one because I had only three of the daisies!

Mohair is used for the covering because it doesn't show the seam. (Neither does an embroidered lace. See number I of this chapter.)

Mark off with your yellow velvet ribbon the three equidistant sections, but do *not* glue it yet. The purpose of this procedure is to let you determine accurately at what spot to hang the gold chain. Cut three equal lengths of the chain, long enough to fall gracefully at the center of the ball. Secure each side of the chain. With your ice pick, make two shallow holes at the point you have selected at the edge of the yellow ribbon. Place a small hairpin over a link of the chain and insert into the ball. Ditto for the opposite side: Secure the end of the chain at the same height as the first end. Repeat the procedure on the two remaining thirds of the ball.   **Step 1**

Now glue on your inch-wide yellow velvet ribbon.   **Step 2**

Apply the cording. This one is a curly white silk with a gold thread running through.   **Step 3**

Apply the "filigree" gold sequins at equidistant points over the white cording.   **Step 4**

Secure the flower (white, yellow, and green) just above the golden chain. Apply glue to the back of it; insert pins unobtrusively.   **Step 5**

The bottom decoration consists of two leaves (like those on the flowers), a white "pearl," a faceted green crystal bead, a quite large white bead, an avocado-green-headed corsage pin.

91

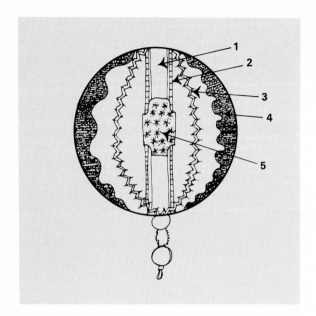

Here you see the two rhinestone clips (from my friend's black velvet
dress) which, but for my intervention, would have graced the hospital thrift
shop! (See Chapter "What You'll Need and Where to Get It.")

The covering is fire-engine red velvet.

Step 1   Apply the inch-wide white velvet ribbon to only the two opposite seams
of the ball. (The other two seams will be of something else. See *Step 4* below.)

Step 2   The sides of the velvet ribbon are beaded: silver bugle beads.

Step 3   Apply the narrow white braid which is edged, here and there, in silver.

Step 4   Apply the wide rope of silver sequins on the two remaining seams.

Step 5   Those blessed clips! Glue on backside. Secure with pins, top and bottom.

The bottom decoration consists of a large white "pearl," a faceted red
bead, another large white "pearl," two red crystal beads — on a
white corsage pin.

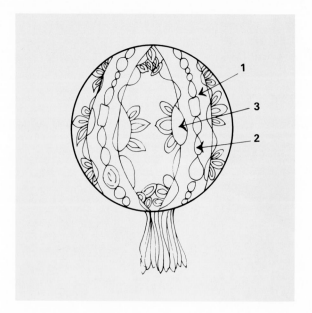

The covering is avocado green felt.

Step 1   One-inch rosy red velvet ribbon is applied over the four seams.

Step 2   Because the beads here are of varying shapes and kinds, they are cumbersome to handle; so I advise you to bead each of the four sides with four separate wires, rather than the usual two. After you have finished one string of the beading, secure it in a straight line by putting gold-headed pins on both sides of, say, a large gold bead. These won't show. They will keep the line from wobbling!

Step 3   Apply this handsome yellow and gold braid.

The bottom decoration is simply a hank of gold beads.

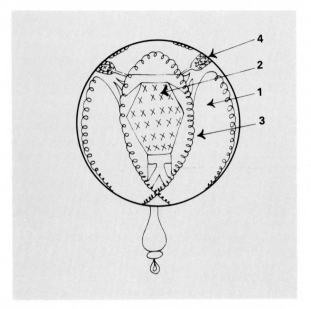

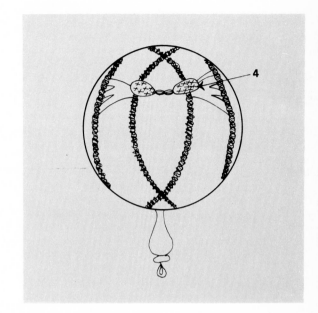

V

Side 1   Side 2

This number (see Chapter "What You'll Need and Where to Get It") was inspired by the elderly neighbor's old shoes which were about to be hauled off to the incinerator. Don't you agree that they date, at the very least, back to the F. Scott Fitzgerald era? At the time of my seizing upon them (along with a falling-apart but heavily beaded georgette dress), I didn't know just *how* they could be used; but I had the conviction that they could, in some mysterious way, glamorize something. This is still another example showing that you can always use something beautiful. No problem except to invent the how!

The covering is white wool mohair.

An inch-and-a-half-wide avocado green velvet ribbon is applied over the seams of half the ball; a 1½-inch-wide burgundy velvet ribbon over the two opposite seams.   **Step 1**

The silver leather thong is applied.   **Step 2**

A silver roping outlines the sides of the velvet ribbons. (This roping has a tendency to "roll"; secure it here and there with pins.)   **Step 3**

To conceal the buttonholes on the sides of the thongs, as well as to add a lovely decoration to the otherwise undecorated remaining two quarters, I applied two rhinestone links from a bracelet. Simply glue on backside of same and secure with pins here and there.   **Step 4**

The bottom decoration is from an old hatpin; then a silver "pearl." A white "pearl" corsage pin is used to harmonize with the white mohair covering.

The decorated Christmas trees never fail to elicit paeans of admiration. The ones illustrated here are made from conical-shaped styrofoam 11½ inches high, 12½ inches in circumference at the base. (They come in other sizes as well.) Decorate them in a horizontal style (numbers I and III) or in a vertical one. The horizontal style needs no primary covering of the styrofoam. Their glamour belies their simplicity.

Three trees are illustrated here, but there are as many variations in design for the trees as there are for the other ornaments illustrated in this book. Look at your trimmings and determine what color combinations will heighten the décor of your rooms.

The tree and base require a greater quantity of trimmings than the balls. So before you start one, check to see that you have an adequate supply of same. The three trees shown here are set directly on a decorated base of styrofoam. Scale the size of your base to the dimensions of your tree. The bases shown here are six-inch circles cut from a sheet of styrofoam which you can obtain from your wholesale florist. Use a key hole saw to cut them out. Another style is to make a "trunk" of the tree by inserting one end of a length of wooden dowel (gilded gold or silver, or painted) into the middle of the bottom of the tree, the other end of the dowel into the middle of the base.

I

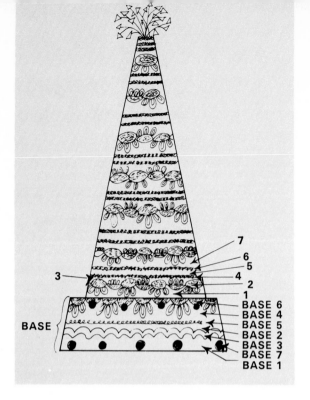

The grouping of colors here is really way-out, making for a startling "mod" effect: Kelly green tinsel ribbon, blue tinsel ribbon, bright orange satin ribbon, narrow light blue silk braid, single strands of cerise sequins, Kelly green sequins, brilliant blue sequins, and a bright yellow baroque swag braid. (See Chapter "Midas's Touch": This gorgeous braid was white originally. I dyed it!)

Since sequins the same color as the tinsel ribbon wouldn't be seen were they to be superimposed on the ribbon, the cerise or blue are applied to the green ribbon; the green or cerise on the blue, etc.

Tree

Step 1   Green tinsel ribbon.
Step 2   Yellow braid.
Step 3   Orange satin ribbon.
Step 4   Cerise sequins.
Step 5   Narrow sky blue braid.
Step 6   Green sequins.
Step 7   Blue tinsel ribbon.

Repeat the "steps" up to the top.

Base

Step 1   Blue tinsel ribbon.
Step 2   Orange satin ribbon.
Step 3   Narrow roping of Kelly green sequins.
Step 4   Two rows of the narrow sky blue braid.
Step 5   Cerise sequins.
Step 6   Yellow braid.

Step 7   Very large "pearls" of a goldish cast (on gold-headed pin) are applied at equidistant points on the bottom of the blue tinsel ribbon; the "pearls" at the top of the base are staggered between the bottom ones.

The top decoration is several bunches of yellow gold beads twisted together and inserted.

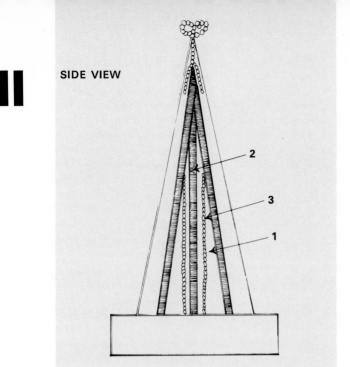

SIDE VIEW

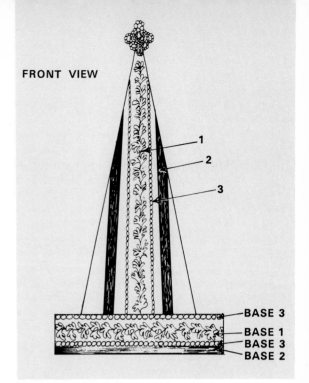

FRONT VIEW

Tree

See "Pattern for Cloth of Gold Covering." (See sketch of side view.) Cut two of these and apply them to opposite sides of the styrofoam.	**Step 1**
A line of sky blue velvet ribbon down the center of this Cloth of Gold covering.	**Step 2**
A band of blue sequins is applied about one-quarter inch from each side of the velvet ribbon.	**Step 3**
A 1½-inch-wide gold ribbon embroidered with sky blue leaves is applied to the center of the two remaining sides of the styrofoam. (See sketch of front view.)	**Step 1**
A band of the blue sequins is applied on the edges of the ribbon.	**Step 2**
Velvet ribbon is applied about one-quarter inch from each outer side of the two bands of sequins.	**Step 3**

Base

Covering: Cut two circles of the Cloth of Gold, allowing for a bit to go over the edges of the base.

Apply the embroidered gold ribbon.	**Step 1**
The blue velvet ribbon at the bottom of the base.	**Step 2**
A band of the blue sequins on both sides of the embroidered gold ribbon.	**Step 3**

Top Decoration: A series of circles in which are used beads of the same colors incorporated in the tree and base. A detailed explanation for making same is found in Chapter "Make Your Own Thing."

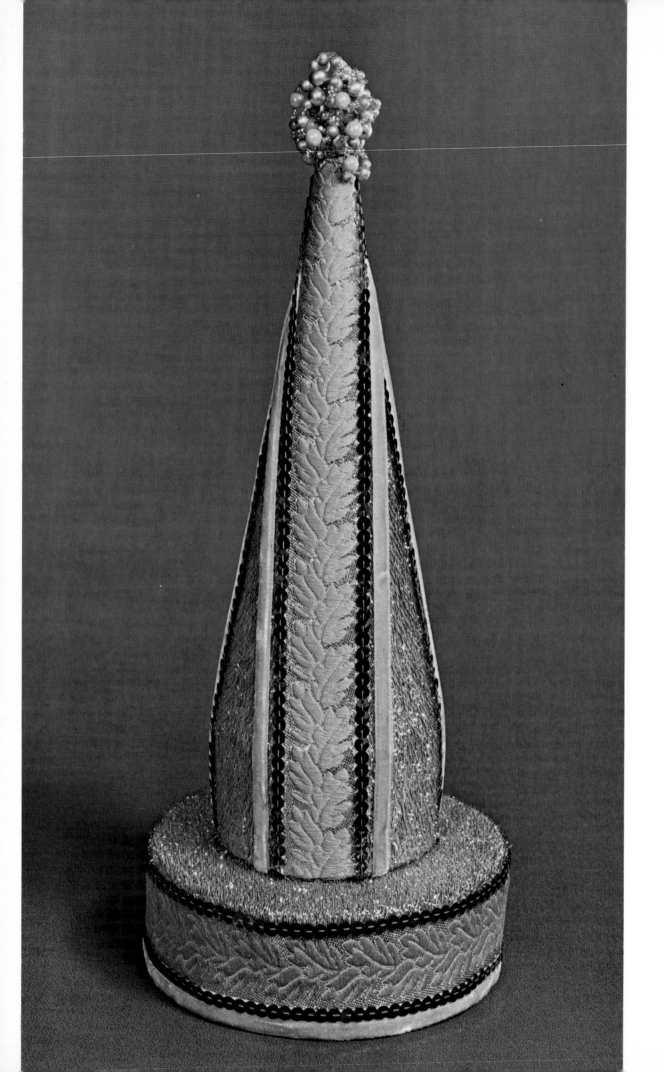

Pattern for Cloth of Gold
covering. "Tannenbaum" II.
(Approximately 4½ inches at the base;
8½ inches high.)

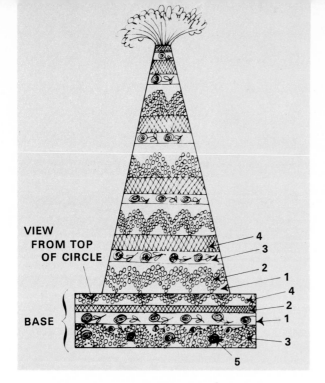

VIEW
FROM TOP
OF CIRCLE

BASE

This one is very simple to make. It's the combination of colors and textures which give it its effectiveness.

Step 1   An inch-and-a-half-wide mod-pink velvet ribbon.

Step 2   Superimposed on the ribbon is a wide roping of rose sequins.

Step 3   A blue silk ribbon embroidered in roses of pink, rose, cerise with green stems and leaves.

Step 4   A three-quarter-inch avocado green velvet ribbon.

Start again with *Step 1* and repeat steps up to the top.

Base

Covering: The base is covered in a mod-pink loosely woven wool. (A stretchy material is used for this purpose because any other, such as velvet, satin, felt, etc., would pucker when pulled over the sides of the circle.)

Cut two circles of this covering, the size of the base, plus an extra inch or so for good measure. Apply one circle of the cloth to the top and one to the bottom. The trimmings will cover the raw edges of the material.

Step 1   Two rows of the blue embroidered ribbon are applied. The first one is seen in the dip in the curve of the sequin roping and the second fully seen.

Step 2   A narrow avocado green velvet ribbon is at the top of the base.

Step 3   Apply the rose sequin roping at the bottom of the base.

Step 4   Viewing the base from the top: Apply the sequin roping so that the bottom of the curve of the roping meets the top of the velvet ribbon.

Step 5   At equidistant points at the very bottom of the base: an iridescent large rose-colored "pearl" through which is stuck a pink corsage pin. (These large "pearls" were "pop beads." Cut off the little tail by which they were connected, one to the other. Pierce a hole in the tail's place. And there you have it!)

Top Decoration: The clusters of little avocado green beads are "store-bought." For making the circles of rose-colored crystal beads, green bugle beads, rose-colored bugle beads, and tiny blue beads — all the colors incorporated in the tree and base — see Chapter "Make Your Own Thing."

N ow, Decorate Yourself for Christmas

If you are sick and tired of the plastic mistletoe, the sprig of holly, and the shaggy Santa as Christmas decorations for your person, do something about it.

Take a look in your costume-jewelry drawer and get out the eardrops that you no longer wear. Clip-ons or the old screw-ons lend themselves equally well for your purpose. You have a lot of fun in store!

Set them out in a row beside your scraps of fabrics, have a look at your trimmings, and select the colors that harmonize with each pair. You'll want to make several pair of them for yourself (what are the colors in the costumes you plan to wear during the holidays?) and you'll be giving some as gifts. In addition to making some for the members of your family, take a pair to your hostess of a merry holiday party.

Call her in advance and ask the color of the dress she'll be wearing. "No," you say, "I don't plan on sending you a corsage, Dearie!" Then starts a guessing-game, but don't give in! If she won't tell you, take her a pair in a safe color: green, red, or white, with its gold or silver trimmings! They're not only beautiful, they're amusing. Both you and they will be sensational! They are something really different for the woman who has everything! You can bet your life that she doesn't have a pair of these.

They're quick and easy to make: Just use the same basic techniques as for the other ornaments illustrated elsewhere in this book. Often you won't need to cut a pattern from fabric for the covering of the styrofoam because one ribbon and one braid can cover the little ball. (See I, II, IV, and V of this chapter.) But if you have a fabric which you especially like and want to use, the pattern for the covering is on the first page of the Chapter "Ready? Go!"

There are several sizes of these little styrofoam balls offered in the five-and-dime stores as well as in the mail-order catalogues. The ones shown here are, I believe, 1½ inch. There is a smaller size, too, on the market.

If the eardrop is simply "gold" or "silver" or "diamonds," you'll be at liberty to use any colors you fancy. If the eardrop is a definite color, choose the materials which harmonize with it.

There is only one step in the making of these which differs from the other ornaments illustrated in this book and that one is the inserting of the eardrop: Make two very shallow holes with your ice pick through the ribbons and braids at the top. Dip the ends of the little hairpin in glue. Now slip your eardrop through the hairpin. Apply a bit more glue to the hairpin (but *not* all the way to the top of it). Push the hairpin down to the depth which allows freedom for the eardrop to work and allows your decorated ball to hang straight.

It may be that the ends of the hairpin protrude through the bottom of your decoration. No problem. Just snip off those ends flush with the styrofoam ball you've decorated.

If you want to use your original eardrops after the holidays (they may be ones you like to wear throughout the year), no problem here either! The ball you've decorated is easily removed from your eardrops without disturbing anything: simply use your ice pick to raise the hairpin a bit and slip out your originals. Leave the hairpin *up* so that you can slip your eardrops in again for next year's holidays: use a "twee" of glue and push back down.

Attractive eardrops are always in abundance at the "outlets" mentioned in the Chapter "What You'll Need and Where to Get It." They go for little or nothing, usually ten cents or fifteen cents. Pick up plenty of them so that you'll have a selection from which to choose. They're really fun to make.

The following ten illustrations give you a look at the limitless variations which you can adopt or adapt to concoct these eye-catching "people decorations."

The eardrops themselves are gold with an "emerald" in the center; rhinestones surround the outer edge of the gold.

Two strips of ribbon (cerise pleated satin) cross the ball in opposite directions. — **Step 1**

A nubby narrow gold metallic braid edges the ribbon. — **Step 2**

Two strips of very narrow emerald green sequin roping. — **Step 3**

No bottom decoration. (Don't you agree that there's quite enough decoration as is? No point in piling it on!)

Hairpin: Put the fastener of the eardrop through the hairpin.

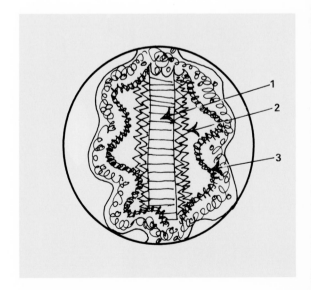

This pair of eardrops has a faceted jet "jewel" at its center; two concentric rings of rhinestones surround it.

Step 1   Two strips of white ribbon embroidered in silver cover the ball.

Step 2   Two strips of very narrow black velvet ribbon.

Step 3   A lacy silver Christmas ribbon (which has been cut down the middle) is on either side of the velvet.

The bottom decoration is a small faceted jet "jewel," such as appears in the original eardrop. Beneath that is a rondure of rhinestones. (If a large "jewel" is applied to the bottom of the ball, you'll have to lengthen the space between your earlobe and your shoulder!)

Hairpin: Eardrop through it.

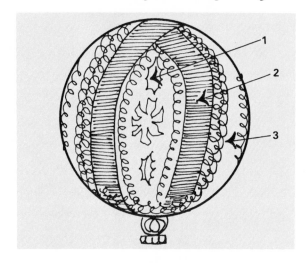

The eardrop is a series of gold leaves; a gold "pearl" is in the center.
The covering is a loosely woven hot pink wool.

Apply a narrow gold ribbed ribbon over the seam-coverings.   Step 1

The bright yellow braid around the circumference of the ball.   Step 2

An electric blue silk cording atop the braid.   Step 3

A hot pink sequin on a gold sequin pin is applied over the blue cording   Step 4
(for concealing the beginning and ending ends) and ditto on the yellow braid.
These two sequins are applied at the point where
the braid and cording have been superimposed on
the gold ribbon.

Bottom Decoration: An electric blue small crystal
bead, a tiny gold bead on a gold-headed pin.
Hairpin: Eardrop through it.

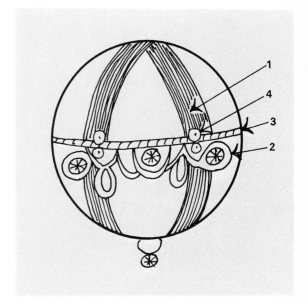

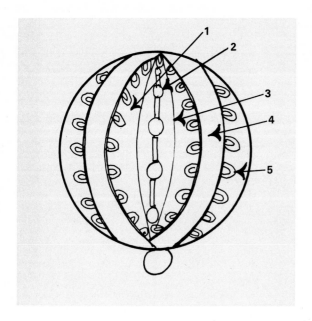

IV

The eardrops are a large "pearl" with a curlicue of rhinestones.

Step 1   Two strips of red velvet ribbon cover the little ball.

Step 2   The beading is a green bugle bead, a "pearl," a bugle bead, rhinestone, bugle bead, "pearl," bugle bead, rhinestone, bugle bead.

Step 3   Silver metallic thread borders the center beading.

Step 4   Two strips of narrow avocado green velvet ribbon.

Step 5   Narrow silver braid borders the velvet ribbon.

The bottom decoration is a "pearl."
Hairpin: Eardrop through it.

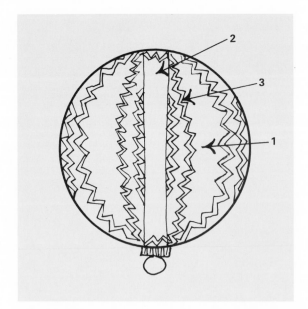

V

The eardrops themselves are silver and "diamonds."

Step 1   Two strips of navy blue grosgrain ribbon.

Step 2   Two strips of cerise pleated satin ribbon. (See I, this chapter.)

Step 3   Two rows of silver baby rickrack border the cerise satin ribbon.

The bottom decoration is a rondure of rhinestones and a silver bead.
Hairpin: Eardrop through it.

The eardrop is gold, amber "jewels," and rhinestones.
The covering is lime green felt.

Step 1   A narrow gold braid covers the seams.

Step 2   A curlicue braid is applied in the middle of each quarter.
(What could be easier?)

No bottom decoration except for a large gold sequin which covers the endings of the curlicue braid.
Hairpin: Eardrop through it.

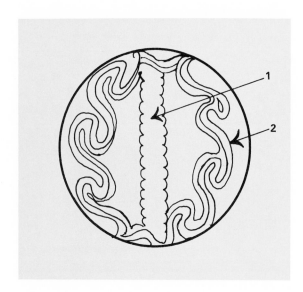

VII

The eardrops are silver, little rhinestones, and marquise-shaped blue crystal. (Let's call them "sapphires"!)

The covering is hot pink loosely woven wool.

A length of narrow blue velvet covers two of the four seams; the other two are covered with orange velvet ribbon. **Step 1**

A narrow curved white braid flecked with silver borders the blue and the orange velvet ribbons. **Step 2**

Bottom Decoration: A bead made up of rhinestones.
Hairpin: Eardrop through it.

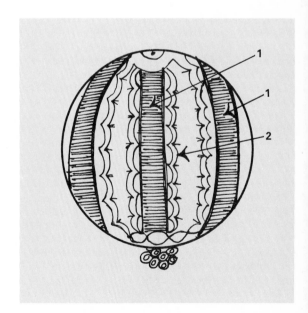

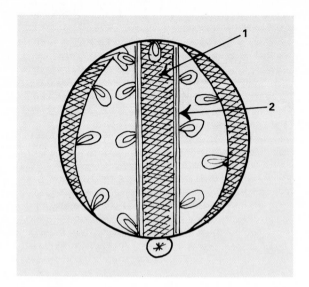

The eardrop is a rosy pink ceramic rose and green leaves mounted on gold metal; rhinestones are at the top.

The covering is a nubby white cloth (a scrap of upholstery material).

Step 1   Two lengths of narrow rosy pink velvet ribbon cover the seams.

Step 2   A gold braid borders the velvet ribbon.

Bottom Decoration: A small gold "pearl."
Hairpin: Eardrop through it.

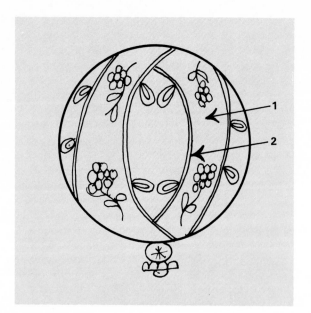

IX

The eardrop is a circle of avocado green crystal beads.
The covering is avocado green felt.

Step 1   The seam-covering is yellow ribbon embroidered in red roses and green leaves and stem.

Step 2   A narrow gold braid borders the ribbon.

The bottom decoration is a gold "pearl" and a large gold and yellow sequin. *Hairpin:* Eardrop through it.

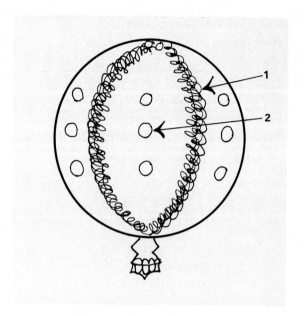

X

The eardrop is faceted red crystal beads.
The covering, white satin embroidered in gold.

Step 1   A fancy curlicue red braid covers the seams.

Step 2   Three red rhinestones in each quarter.

The bottom decoration is a faceted red crystal bead and a gold metal "canopy." (These are frequently found on costume jewelry.)
Hairpin: Eardrop through it.

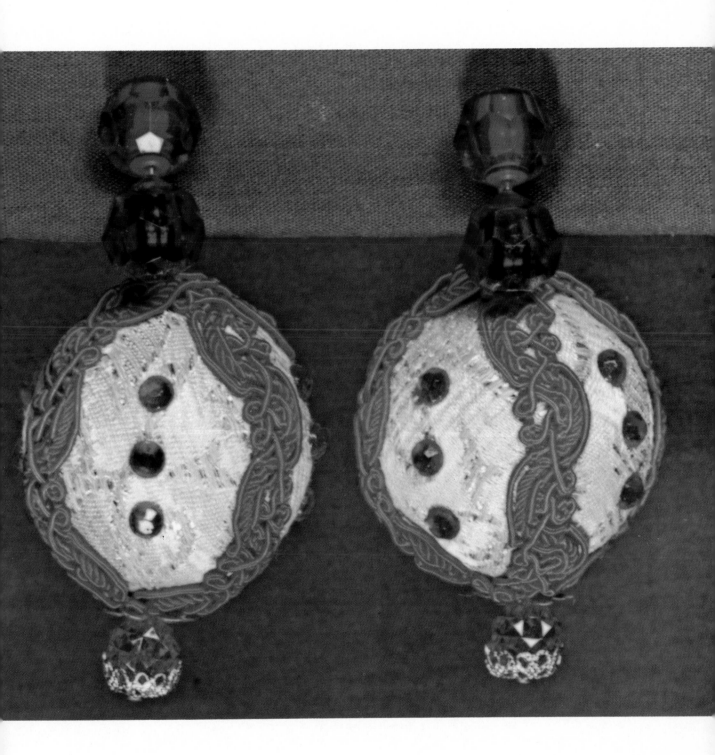

For the Younger Set and for the Handicapped

Children of all ages get a big charge out of making a gift for their parents. "I made it just for you, Mom, and all by myself. And I made this one for you, Daddy." The making of a simple yet effective Christmas ornament is a great project for a group of any kind: for a class at school, at Sunday school, for a Brownie or Girl Scout group, for Rainbow Girls, etc.

The making of these decorations is a great project for "special" schoolers as well as welcomed therapy for the physically and/or emotionally handicapped at rehabilitation centers and hospitals. If the rehabilitation center has plans for a Christmas Bazaar, start making them well in advance. Make them in quantity because they always sell like hotcakes! These patients certainly needn't confine themselves to the very simple ones such as outlined in this chapter. Have a look at some of the others.

You're no doubt asking: "Who's going to pay for the necessary materials?" Well, that's never a problem: If for a class at school, the cost of the styrofoam and "findings" can very probably come out of the school's art department budget. Or, if for a Sunday school class or a Brownie group, etc., there's almost always a "sinking fund" or "petty cash" somewhere around to pay the few dollars which the various materials will cost. However, if for any reason there's a hassle about having the cash forthcoming, each child can certainly bring, say, seventy-five cents or a dollar from his/her family for the very important and very secret present to be made.

As for the money required in the rehabilitation centers, hospitals, or "special" schools, there's always a fund set aside for expenditures necessary for providing therapy. And the suggestion for this specific project will be welcomed with open arms.

To avoid chaos, have the entire group of youngsters use the same materials and make the same design. Were there to be variations on the theme, the teacher of the group would no doubt end up in the looney-bin. The procedure is: "Now we cut the so-and-so. Now we glue the so-and-so." All members must complete one step before the next step is undertaken.

The teacher must, of course, make a model in advance so as to be certain of the steps and techniques of the procedures. By this, she will, as well, be able to determine the required number of yards of covering, of braid or inexpensive ribbon, the "pearls" or sequins or buttons, the pins and hairpins, or whatever is to be used. For the young folks, she will put into individual cellophane bags: the paper pattern to be used for cutting the four quarters of covering; the braid or ribbon cut into the required lengths; the needed sequins or "jewels"; on down to the pins and hairpin.

As for the inserting of the hairpin at the top, since an ice pick can be a lethal weapon, the teacher, upon completion of the decorating, will have to be the one to start the hairpin: Make the two shallow holes through the braid or ribbon covering the seams. The hairpin is then to be dipped in glue and inserted.

For attaching the card (see Chapter "Helps" — Cards), I think that the last of the suggestions given there is the most appropriate for the younger set: String a metallic thread through a hole punched out in the card, knot, string the metallic thread through the hairpin and tie a bow: "To Mother. Christmas 19__. Love, Sue."

The teacher will, of course, determine just how far up the ladder she can go with the decorating. Her guideline is the age and capabilities of her group.

Following are three models, all quite simple to execute. If the group is made up of older and therefore more capable children, the teacher could well select models from the many others illustrated between these covers.

I

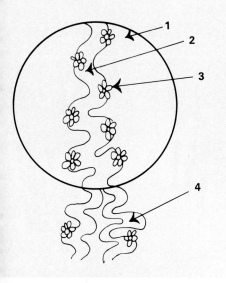

The following three ornaments have only four steps: from the covering of the ball through the bottom decoration.

Cover the ball with the fabric of your choice. (The covering here is nylon blue velvet. But velvets and satins are not the easiest materials to handle. Felt or woolens are the easiest.)   **Step 1**

Cover the seams of the four quarters with a flashy braid or ribbon. (The one here is wide silver rickrack.)   **Step 2**

Put a "jewel" or a fancy button here and there on the braid or ribbon. (The ball in the illustration has a blue plastic flower, secured by a silver sequin on a pin, at each of the curves of the silver rickrack.)   **Step 3**

The bottom decoration in the illustration is two equal lengths of the silver rickrack, crossing each other, and secured by the blue plastic flower and a silver sequin on a pin. At the four ends of the rickrack have been sewn, with invisible nylon thread, a flower and a silver sequin. The teacher will judge the capabilities of her group: If it isn't quite up to handling the bottom decoration as shown here, a large blue or silver bead could serve in its place.   **Step 4**

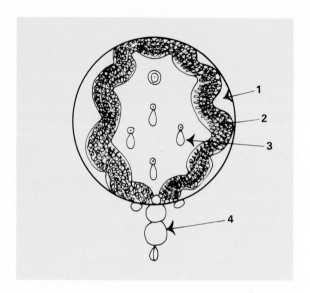

Step 1   Cover the ball with fabric. The one shown here is lime green felt.

Step 2   Cover the seams with braid or ribbon. (The covering in the illustration has a wide rope of Kelly green sequins, but I certainly don't recommend young children's using this. Even single strands of sequins aren't the easiest trimming in the world to handle. But for older children or for adults, yes.)

Step 3   The four spaces between the seam–covering can be decorated with various-shaped single large sequins (they come in the shape of shells, snowflakes, stars, and dozens of others) or with beads of a color to harmonize or to contrast with the braid or ribbon used over the seams, or by a glittery button in the middle of the quarter. Secure the button by glue on the backside; and in the holes of the button, a sequin on pins which have been dipped in glue. (The decoration here in each quarter is a single "pearl" over a green sequin; and below it, four drop "pearls" which have a wire loop at their top. The "pearl" is secured by a green sequin and a pin which has been dipped in glue.)

Step 4   For the bottom decoration, a large bead to harmonize with the colors used on the ornament. (The bottom decoration here is a large baroque "pearl," a large green crystal bead, a "pearl" corsage pin.)

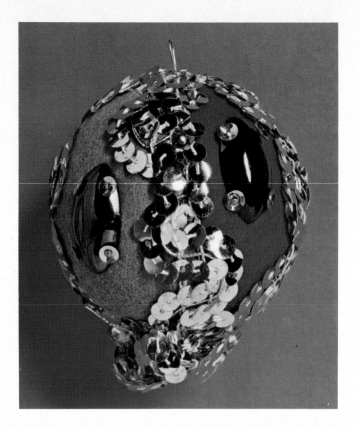

Step 1	Cover the ball with fabric. The one here in the illustration has two of the quarters covered in a light blue felt; the opposite quarters in magenta felt.
Step 2	Cover the seams with your attractive braid or ribbon. (The seam-covering in the illustration is, again, a wide rope of sequins; but, again, this trimming is tricky to work with and I don't recommend it for the very young or the inept; so, better to use an attractive substitute.)
Step 3	The center decoration is simple indeed: one large iridescent sequin in the center of each quarter, secured by four pins on which has been put a silver sequin.
Step 4	You could use the same large sequin for the bottom finish (or use four of them: one at the base of each of the four seam-coverings) as has been used in the center of each quarter.

P.S. See also number V of the Chapter "Without Benefit of Bangles."
What could be simpler to make than this one?
If the group is not old enough or capable enough to handle the gluing of a single strand of sequins, substitute a narrow plain silver or blue ribbon in its stead.

Midas's Touch

It isn't always possible to find the desired color in appropriate ornamentations. For example, I came across a hundred or so of tiny oval "frames" which I knew would be just the ticket for ringing a "jewel" (see "Some Stylish Models" IX) in order to give it added importance, but these "frames" were black, a color which is scarcely usable. Another crop of tiny "frames" was copper-colored circles. I left a few dozen of the copper-colored ones as they were, to be used when decorating with yellows or coppery tones of ornamentation; but the remainder of these, along with all the black ones, underwent a coloring job.

I put them on the tops of corrugated boxes (get several from your grocery store or bottle shop), held them in place with four pins (top and bottom, outer edge and inner edge), and applied gilt to some and silver to others. I used them dozens of times and they indeed carried out their purpose of enhancing the ornamentation. As you can see by the illustrations, these "frames" emphasize the attractiveness and importance of the "jewel" which they surround.

Similarly, I came across what appeared to be literally thousands of quite large sequins in all colors and in many designs (snowflakes, stars, shells, oblongs, circles, squares). I sorted out the usable, attractive colors from the whites, greys, washed-out pinks, etc. I gilded or painted these latter nondescript colors to my own order and was delighted to be able to call on them many a time for a variety of uses: under "jewels" in my center-of-the-quarter decoration (again, for the purpose of embellishing a "jewel," see "Be Two-Faced" IV) at the top and/or bottom as a "finish"; for necessary concealment of ribbons' or braids' cut ends; and in between the "jewels" of the bottom decoration (the tail) where certainly the usual size of sequin would go unnoticed. (See "Some Stylish Models" XII.)

Often you can pick up a whole card of lace in junk shops or at white elephant sales for little or nothing. Get it and gild it! It makes a handsome trimming. Simply pin it here and there on a box top and get out your gilts!

"Pearl" necklaces and bracelets are always offered in abundance at the many "outlets" and they go for pennies. (Broken strands of "pearls" are sometimes found at white elephant sales.) You will need only a certain percentage of "pearls" in their original pearl state. So, gild them gold or paint them silver or apply several colors you like. (A brand named "Daz-L" is one I use. The

colors are brilliant, even psychedelic. Go to your paint store and have a look around!)

You can undo the strings of "pearls" and paint them by sticking them on a pin; or you can secure the entire string on your corrugated box top, pinning it here and there (outer and inner sides) in order to hold it securely. Stick a few extra pins into your box top and put a dot of your gilt or paint on their heads so that they're ready to use when needed. The gold-headed pins will be particularly in demand as you go about your craft.

While you're gilding or painting, stick a few dozen of your corsage pins into the box top and give them the business because you will be needing gold and silver and colored ends. (I have never come across a gold or silver corsage pin and so have always gilded or colored my own.)

Incidentally, I always take a good look around before I start my color changing so as to be sure that I've gathered absolutely everything I want to color in order to do the whole works at one time. This method saves time for your really creative labors.

Sometimes, the things which you have gilded or colored will need a second coat. If so, don't clean your brushes right away. Instead, put them in a little glass of turpentine or varnoline for use the following day. Again, economize on your time. Save it for your creativity.

Silken braids can be dyed and laces, too. Hanks of straw braid or horsehair braid can be gilded or painted or dyed. If you do not find the colors of braids which please you, select a very light color or white; cut off lengths of a few yards each and dye them. Get a box of dye in each of the three primary colors (red, blue, yellow). First, dye several lengths in varying degrees of intensity of each of the primary colors. (As you know, the degree of intensity of the color is determined by the length of time your braids, etc., remain in the dye-bath.) Then mix some of the red and the blue to get lavender and purple; some of the red and yellow to get orange; some blue and yellow to get green. This process takes only minutes and will give you an endless variety of colors from which you can choose.

If you come across a braid quite handsome in design but blah in color, it can be safely dyed. See number I of the Chapter "Tannenbaum." When I happened upon this gorgeous braid in a bin of odds and ends at a church bazaar, it was an oyster white and quite soiled. I washed it gently and then dyed some of it a golden yellow and some a bright green. It has filled the bill for many a decoration. And if I recall correctly, its price tag read: "$2.00 — 18 yds." Its price to me was eleven cents per dirty yard . . . but look at it now! A first-rate face-lift, wouldn't you say? Conclusion: Being an imaginative scavenger pays off!

![M]ake Your Own Thing—Circles and Canopies

It could happen that no matter how many "jewels" you have in your storehouse, none lends itself to the effect you want to create. Then, why not make your own?

Following are some suggestions on how you can use your talents to create some "jewels" or to enhance some which you have on hand. Make circles and "canopies" in appropriate sizes (scale them to the size of the ornament or "jewel") and in varying color combinations. The step-by-step instructions for making same are given below.

You can use the circles on the bottom of an ornament as a base in order to permit it to stand up. (See Chapter "Sitting Ducks.") Or make these circles or "canopies" out of tiny beads to apply to the ball itself, and place a "jewel" inside them. Thus, they will "ring" the "jewel" and give it added importance. For these tiny ones, use your fine wire. The "jewel" in the center will hide the ends of this wire. For making the circles as bases or for top decorations of your Christmas trees, use your floral wire. (See numbers II and III of Chapter "Tannenbaum.") Had these top decorations been made with fine wire, they would flop down instead of standing erect.

The "canopies" can likewise be used as a base on the bottom of a ball (see Chapter "Sitting Ducks," numbers II and IV) or simply as a bottom decoration (see Chapter "Some Stylish Models," numbers IV, X, XIII).

Refer to the Chapter "Tannenbaum." Have a look at the top decoration of number III. My thought was that the "store-bought" clusters of green alone were a bit dull and needed some sprucing up. So I made five separate circles, kept the wires long so that they could be inserted into the styrofoam, twisted together these five circles together with the "store-bought" green clusters, and inserted all at the top. These circles incorporate the colors used on the tree: three bright blue beads, a green bugle bead, a mod-pink bugle bead, a green bugle bead, a faceted mod-pink crystal bead. Repeat the same scheme for the remaining half of the circle. To attach these at the top of the tree, make a little hole with your ice pick, dip the end wires in your glue pot, and insert.

Now have a look at "Tannenbaum," number II. I had nothing ready-made which I considered appropriate for this tree. So I made my own, incorporating the colors used on the tree itself: two sizes of blue "pearls" to match the sky blue embroidery of the gold ribbon; two sizes of gold "pearls." These larger "pearls" are separated (to avoid the decoration from looking heavy) by two tiny gold beads. This top decoration is simply a series of circles twisted together.

I wanted a center which would stand tall and proud. So I cut a wire to a length which would accommodate four or five circles. Push the beads which are to form the first circle to the center of the long wire, and twist; repeat for second circle; repeat until you have the number of circles which suits your taste. The remainder of the top decoration is simply separate, rather large circles twisted (along with the tall center one) together.

Now have a look at the bottom decoration of numbers VII, X, XIII, and XV of Chapter "Some Stylish Models." In number VII, the little "canopy" of tiny gold beads was placed over the large gold "pearl." In number X, I thought that this silver ornament at the bottom was rather stark looking (it was originally the end of a hatpin) and could do with some "softening up"; so I made a "canopy" for it: two red bugle beads, a faceted clear crystal bead; repeat for the other half of the loop, four loops in all. Don't you agree that the "canopy" is quite an enhancement?

On number XIII, each loop of the "canopy" has two tiny "pearls," a silver bugle bead, two tiny "pearls," a green bugle bead, two tiny "pearls," a faceted green crystal bead; repeat for the other half of the loop. On number XV, a "canopy" of tiny gold beads dresses up the large pink "pearl."

On number IV of Chapter "Sitting Ducks," there are two "canopies": the top one, tiny gold beads and green bugle beads; the bottom one, tiny gold beads and blue bugle beads. The ornaments having "canopies" as the bottom decoration can be used to sit or to hang on your tree. Number II of the same chapter has a "canopy" as a bottom decoration incorporating the colors on the ornament itself: tiny pinkish "pearls," cerise bugle beads, lavender bugle beads, lavender "pearls."

How to Make a Circle

Numbers I and II illustrated here are made with large beads and are to be used as bases on the bottom of the ball. (See Chapter "Sitting Ducks.")

Measure how much floral wire is needed to go around the bottom of the ball. Cut off approximately three times this length of wire. If the ball measures six inches around the bottom circumference, your wire will be 18 inches, etc.

The number of beads will be divisible by three or four: 12, 16, etc.

So that there will be no collision of colors, select beads which will harmonize with those on the ornament itself. (Gold or silver are always 100 percent safe.) For making small circles of tiny beads with which to "ring" a "jewel" on the ornament itself, *Steps 5* and *6* in the instructions which follow can be eliminated. Simply go to the opposite side of the circle with the longer wire; twist; return it to the short wire in the center; twist. Apply the "jewel" in the center of the circle, with the pin going through the "jewel" and the little twist of wires in the center.

I

Step 1   The circle begins by using a smallish gold bead, then a large one, then another smallish one. (This will form a quarter of the finished circle.) This procedure will be repeated three more times. There is a total of 12 beads on your wire.

Step 2   Leave two or three inches of the wire free — enough to go to the middle of the circle of beads, plus an extra inch or so. We shall call this short two- or three-inch end (the length of this end is determined by the size of the ball), End *A*; the long end, End *B*.

Step 3   Twist *A* and *B* around each other once in the center of the circle.

Step 4   Take the long wire, *B*, across to the opposite side of the circle. Twist once around the wire on which have been strung the beads. (This leaves an equal number of beads on each half of the circle. Count them to verify.) Bring this long wire back to the center inside the circle. Here, you will twist it around the short end, *A*.

Step 5   Take the long end, *B*, over to the middle of one of the two remaining halves of the circle. Twist it once over the wire on which the beads have been strung, such as was done in *Step 4*. Bring it back to the center. Twist it over the short end, *A*.

Step 6   Repeat *Step 5*, taking the long wire, *B*, to the last remaining half of the circle; twist; take it to the middle; twist around the short wire, *A*, several times. Cut off the excess wire. Apply it to the bottom of the ornament. Conceal the four crossings of wires by sequins on pins which have been dipped in glue.

This making of circles sounds tedious and drawn out; but in reality, nothing could be simpler. You'll agree after you've made your first one.

This circle is for a smaller ball. The procedure is the same as for number I. It has sixteen "pearls" in all.

Step 1   Take the long wire, B, across to middle of opposite side of circle, and twist. You will have eight "pearls" on each half of the circle.

Step 2   Take this long wire, B, to the center of the circle; twist around short wire, A.

Step 3   Take to middle of one of the two remaining halves of circle. This gives you four "pearls" in each quarter of the circle. Twist the long wire around the wire on which the beads have been strung and return it to the center. Twist the two wires together.

Step 4   Repeat above *Step 3* on the remaining half. (There are eight "pearls" here.)

How to Make a "Canopy"

This three-loop "canopy" can be used as a base for an ornament or on the body of a large ornament.

It is a combination of copper-colored beads and gold "pearls." Determine how large you want each loop of the "canopy"; cut off the total length of wire necessary, plus a few extra inches.

On this one are strung on floral wire eight of the copper-colored beads, a gold "pearl," eight copper beads, a gold "pearl," eight copper beads. **Step 1**

Leave an inch or so of wire free. Twist the long end around the short free end. **Step 2**

Repeat this procedure two more times. This gives you a three-loop "canopy." Cut off the excess wire. Secure to the bottom of the ornament as a base, or on the body of the ornament itself with a large gold "pearl" in its center. **Steps 3 and 4**

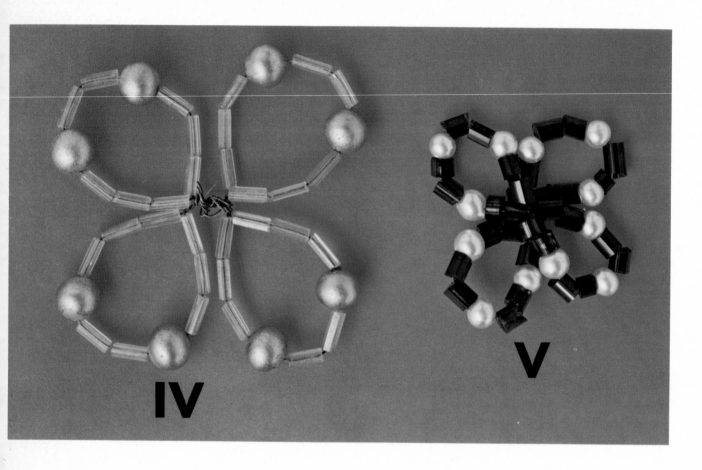

IV

This one is made in exactly the same manner as the preceding one except, of course, you'll be cutting a longer wire because of the extra loop. A "canopy" can be made with as many loops as you judge appropriate. Note the one in Chapter "Kings of the Realm," number I. This little "canopy" of gold beads has six loops because the pink "pearl" in the bottom decoration is quite large. Anything less would look skimpy.

The beads used in this number IV for each loop are three yellow bugle beads, a gold "pearl," two yellow bugle beads, a gold "pearl," three yellow bugle beads.

V

This one is a combination of large purple beads and "pearls": two beads, a "pearl," two beads, a "pearl," two beads, a "pearl," two beads.

VI

A combination of tiny bright blue beads and "pearls": six blue beads, a "pearl," six blue beads, a "pearl," six blue beads, a "pearl," six blue beads.

VII

Each loop in this little one is simply five silver bugle beads.

VIII

In this one, each loop has twelve blue bugle beads. Make two separate "canopies." Superimpose one on top of the other. Twist the wires together. Very showy, isn't it?

(Number IV in Chapter "Sitting Ducks" has two "canopies" also. The top one is made of green bugle beads and tiny gold beads; the bottom one, of blue bugle beads and tiny gold beads.)

Other Ways, Other Uses

There are always picture frames at the outlets mentioned previously: thrift shops, church bazaars, white elephant sales, etc. Pick up a few for yourself. Large-ish ones will best serve your purpose. Either paint the frame a color which will harmonize or contrast with colors you have chosen to use on your ornaments, or gild or silver the frame.

Cut a piece of cardboard (from a corrugated box) to fit onto the back of the frame. Cover the front of it with a rich fabric, i.e., velvet, satin, lamé. Have in mind the color or colors of the ornaments you plan to mount in the frame, and match or contrast sharply with them.

Cut the styrofoam balls in half; decorate; then adhere to the cardboard or corrugated paper with glue and pins.

If you're the least bit bored with the repetitive holly or Dellarobia wreath at your entrance door, hang your own handmade adornments on a wreath of pine at your entrance door. It is best to have a storm door to prevent your creations from being pelted by snow or rain, which would amount to insult. The smaller balls serve best here; otherwise, your storm door may not shut tightly.

Besides Christmas decorations, you can make your own decorations for Easter. The styrofoam comes in an egg shape. Use the same techniques; choose pastel colors, and dainty, frilly, lacy trimmings. And who knows, you

may be judged another Fabergé, the French jeweler who dreamed up the priceless Easter eggs for the Czar's children!

Secure gilded straw matting or colored table mats over the area above the fireplace and mount the half-balls.

A lovely old-fashioned Christmas decoration is to entwine rope-of-pine on the stairway railing. Suspend your Christmas ornaments here and there. Perhaps you will want to tie a ribbon in a bow through the hairpin of the ball, and then suspend the be-ribboned ornaments by the customary hanger.

Use swags or garlands to festoon your bookshelves; or the top of, say, your sideboard; or your chest-on-chest; or your lowboy.

These ornaments are a stunning decoration to a room when hung on the "arms" of a chandelier.

If there are glass panels beside your entrance door, use several here. Hang them in a line, one to the other, by means of invisible nylon string, or by a tinselly ribbon.

The little styrofoam balls on the candelabrum illustrated here are a bit larger than those used to make the eardrops. Choose the size styrofoam ball appropriate in scale for your particular candelabrum or candlesticks.

No need to go into a description of each of these ornaments. Just use the same decorating ideas and techniques on these baby ornaments as have been shown and described in detail for the other ornaments elsewhere in this book.

Note that the only ornaments which have a long bottom decoration are the ones hanging on the first tier. The remainder have simply a small bead, because anything more than that wouldn't permit them to "sit" on their candle cup.

The top ornament has a decoration topside: clusters of gold beads to give the decorated candelabrum a pretty, airy finish.

Candelabra and/or candlesticks decorated with these little ornaments are a lovely touch at holly parties, a wedding buffet or reception, a bachelor's dinner, or a rehearsal dinner at Christmastime. Use several of them to grace the tables of goodies. You may want a combination of candles and your ornaments, or prefer to use the ornaments alone. If black wrought iron doesn't please you, paint or gild the candelabra.

These small ornaments are adorable for decorating a miniature Christmas tree which can be used on a desk, on a table at your picture window, etc. If it's a tiny tree, decorate it with the tiniest size of styrofoam ball. (There are tinier sizes, even, than the one used in making the eardrops. See Chapter "Now Decorate Yourself for Christmas.") These teeny trees can be set on a mantelpiece, a coffee table, kitchen table, even on the tank of the you-know-what in your bathroom.

Once you have the little trees decorated, they can be brought out year after year, all set up. Simply store them as they are in a large cellophane bag. (Don't forget to spray the inside of the bag or to use mothballs!)

the balls themselves or on the corsage pin to form the bottom decoration. (Small beads on the bottom decoration will make the ball resemble a very fat lady who has mockingbird legs!) This principle of "larger at the bottom" seems to give an anchoring effect and is employed in many artistic efforts: i.e., in flower or fruit arrangements, the larger or darker flowers or fruits are at the base of the arrangement. In home decorating, the rug is generally darker than the draperies and wall color. In clothing, skirts are generally darker and of heavier texture than the blouse. (You wouldn't look too chic if your blouse were denim and your skirt organdy.) On this same subject, imagine light pink shoes worn with a rose pink dress. The effect is one of topheaviness. But if the colors of the dress and shoes are reversed, all is coordination, scale, and symmetry.

Varying textures on the same ball give interest: rough with smooth, lacy with plain, etc. This same principle applies in the planning of food combinations: How much more appetizing to serve beets or carrots (rather than mashed turnips) with meat and mashed potatoes. Save the mashed turnips for when you have rice.

Besides making certain that all is secure (you don't want anything falling off the ball or sagging!), be sure that no raw edges show. If there is a likelihood of this, cover the raw edges with appropriate sequins on pins or a bead on a pin or with a "jewel." This concealment measure also heightens decoration.

When you take apart a necklace, bracelet, etc., (this will require the use of pliers or an ice pick), keep the links, etc., together in one box or in a bottle.

Group colors of "jewels" together. It's time-consuming, as well as maddening, to have to look forever for a certain green bead. "I *know* that I have some green crystal beads!" The question is: Where are they? In short, keep yourself organized.

Put your braids, ribbons, cordings, weltings, etc., in transparent cellophane bags. Group them according to category: all weltings grouped together but in separate bags, all cordings together, etc., so that you don't have to go a-hunting.

Put the finished decoration in a cellophane bag and pin it or use a twist-tie. This protects the decorations from one another and, at the same time, keeps them clean.

If you find that a string of beading isn't behaving itself and stubbornly refuses to stay in a straight line, the remedy is to stick a pin (or a bead on a pin) on both sides of the recalcitrant string of "jewels." Often very large or unevenly shaped "jewels" are culprits. Perhaps you will find it necessary to take this remedial measure in two or more places along the string of beading.

You can obtain corsage pins by the box from a wholesale florist.

You'll be using many pins. Ask your tailor or dressmaker to "get them for you wholesale." The little sequin pins and fine wire and floral wire are obtainable at five-and-dime stores.

When you're going to be needing a number of ornamentations for a ball (say, twelve "pearls" atop a "snowflake" sequin; see Chapter "Some Stylish Models" III) assemble all these in advance instead of piecemeal. Stick the twelve "pearls" atop their "snowflake" sequins into a cardboard or, better still, into a piece of styrofoam. This follows the principle of: *Get it all together!*

Some of the seemingly uninteresting plastic jewelry which you may be coming across in your forays can be embellished when properly dressed up with other "jewels" that you have in your storehouse of goodies. Surround the plastic "jewel" with harmonizing or contrasting colors of beads, or put beads on a pin and stick through the openings in the dull plastic. You'll have something surprisingly attractive!

Begin and end a line of beading with small or flat beads (not, say, a "pearl," etc.). Otherwise if your ribbons or braids are on top of, say, a "pearl," the ribbon or braid will be lumpy.

If you happen upon very large sequins, they may, at first glance, look clumsy to you, but get some for yourself. Notice that many of the tops in the illustrations in this book have a large, deep sequin (which I pierced) through which the hairpin was inserted. This large sequin covers any endings which may have been at the top of the ball and, as well, lends added finish.

Hairpins: If you plan to make several sizes of the balls, you'll need the appropriate size of hairpin: tiny ones for eardrops (you may need, moreover, to shorten these, lest they protrude at the bottom of the ball; just put your wire cutters to work); the 2¼-inch hairpin for the 2½-inch and 3-inch balls; and the very heavy 3-inch hairpin for the very large ones ("Kings of the Realm").

Get some "gold" as well as some "silver."

To insert the hairpin, make two very shallow holes (with your ice pick) through the trimmings at the top of the ball — just deep enough to allow the hairpin to get started. Dip the ends of the hairpin in your glue pot; insert, leaving out an adequate length for the hanger.

Beading: Count your first line of bead-design as you go along: "bugle bead, four tiny gold ones, a "pearl," four tiny gold ones, a blue crystal . . . " etc. This will facilitate your beading in the remaining quarters, and all the quarters will be uniform. Otherwise you may end up with, say, some ornaments nearer the top or bottom than the ornaments in the adjacent quarter — which is another way of saying that you'll have a mish-mash.

Glue: Keep your glue in a small plastic medical prescription container whose top can be flipped off. Fit it in the corner of a shallow box, and secure it there by applying glue to the bottom and to two sides of the bottle. You certainly don't want to have to fiddle with unscrewing the original container every time you need glue.

Always keep your brush in a glass of water when you're not using it.

Have a nice, old, absorbent cloth handy to dry your brush before using it again.

If you find that your glue is becoming too thick, stir in a few drops of water.

When you're through for the day, wash your brushes in a mild soap, rinse well in tepid water, press gently between a cloth.

Wire: In beading a center of a quarter, measure how much wire is required to go once around the ball, from top to bottom to top. Add a few extra inches, four or so. Cut as many of these lengths as you'll be needing: If only one line of beading will be in the center of each quarter, cut four lengths. If both sides of a center ribbon or cording are to be beaded, cut eight.

When you begin, secure the wires on the pins. Do it with a slipknot or simply twist the short end — a half inch or so — several times around the long end. Finish by pushing the remainder of the short end toward the head of the pin. Set all of the wires aside, ready for use. Doing ahead of time and all at once a "set" of things which will be needed ("conveyor-belt" style) is a time saver.

If you're beading a large ornament ("Kings of the Realm"), cut enough wire for one quarter only. Because the beads on these are usually larger and therefore unwieldy, it would be cumbersome to try to handle more than one-quarter of the ball at the time.

For these large decorations, as well as for "rings" and "canopies" for the bottom decoration (see Chapter "Make Your Own Thing"), use floral wire instead of the very fine wire. (This is called milliners' wire.) This floral wire is sturdier and therefore stays put better.

Security: You want to make very sure that everything stays where it's supposed to!

When you're pinning on a "jewel," etc., remember to dip the pin in glue.

If a lace or braid refuses to adhere, secure it by putting a sequin or bead on a pin. Place these here and there on your lace or braid or whatever. They serve a dual purpose: They secure your trimming and also add an extra touch of attractiveness to your decoration.

Center Decoration: When your plan is to place an ornament within the line of beading (a link of a bracelet or necklace, a glittery button, a fancy pin, etc. – you'll find illustrations of this plan throughout the book), place this ornament on the ball and mark the space, top and bottom, with pins or by a pencil dot.

Start your beading. As you approach the top pin or the pencil dot, take out the top pin. Place it in what is the center of the space to be left vacant. Wind your beading wire once around this pin; insert fully.

Now continue your beading from the bottom marking point to the bottom of the quarter. Before you wind your wire around the pin at the bottom of the quarter, check that you have left enough room in the center to accommodate your central ornamentation. Otherwise, it won't be lying flat.

My suggestion is that you *not* apply the center decoration until *after* you've completed all the decorating of the ball. This center decoration, if applied immediately, will be in your way as you go about the remaining steps of the decoration, i.e., applying the cording, metallic thread, braids, ribbons. You'll find its largeness and protrusion cumbersome.

Concerning the applying of "frames" (see Chapter "Some Stylish Models" IX and Chapter "Be Two-Faced" II and III), you be your own judge: You can either glue the "frames" on the four quarters before you start the beading (they must, of course, all be equidistant from the top); or do the beading and leave adequate space to apply the "frames" and a "jewel" in the center after you've finished the beading.

Pearls: You'll find that "pearls" have many different hues. Some are pure white, others have a goldish cast or a pinkish cast or are greyish. Because you'll want "pearls" of the same cast on the same ball, don't dump all your "pearls" together. Keep them in separate bottles, according to their cast.

"Pearls" which are to be changed from their original state are easier to gild if kept on their string.

If you have loose "pearls" that you want to gild or paint, string them on floral wire. Put this on a cardboard box, or better still, on a sheet of styrofoam if you have same. Secure on inner side and outer side with pins. (See "Midas's Touch.")

Sequins: Wind your sequin roping and your single strings of sequins on a piece of cardboard so that they don't tangle.

Metallic Thread: When you buy metallic thread, ask the salesperson for a piece of cardboard, and as she measures it off, you wind it on the cardboard.

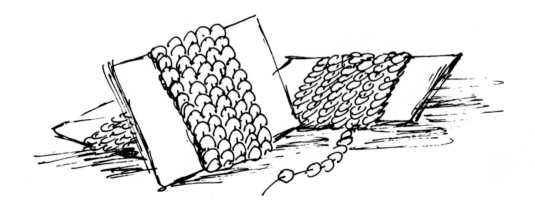

I remember spending half a day untangling and unknotting 100 yards of silver metallic thread which the salesperson had simply put in a paper bag.

Buttons: You'll be coming across many a pretty button which you can use to embellish your decorations.

If the button has the customary two or four holes, simply apply glue to its backside and put a "pearl" (or whatever you choose) on a pin and insert through the holes.

Then, there are buttons with open-work somewhere. Simply secure by means of several pins through this filigree.

And then there are buttons with no openings at all, the ones which were meant to be sewn on clothes from the underneath side. They have a protrusion underneath (with a hole through which the thread was to pass). To apply these buttons to your decorations, make a hole in the ball with your ice pick or scissors just large enough (barely large enough, so that you have to force the button a bit) to accommodate this underneath protrusion. Your button will thus lie flat when applied.

Pins: Don't use more pins than are actually needed — not with the idea of economizing money-wise but of economizing time-wise. Do some advance planning. For example, if there's a possibility that a pin which you've used to secure a cording or welting could be used *also* on which to wind your metallic thread (or whatever), don't insert it fully until it has no remaining purpose to serve. Leave one-fourth inch or so free. Don't apply glue on pins until you're sure they have no further purpose to serve.

The same pins which you've used for the beading-wire can perhaps serve to be the pins to anchor some other trimming as you go along.

Briefly, let one pin do more than one job.

When you're beading, wind wire once around a pin at the bottom of that quarter. You don't need to stick another pin into the bottom of the opposite quarter which may be one-fourth inch away. *However*, when you get to the top of the quarters you will need a pin in their four centers. And when you've completed the beading, wind the wire around two or three of those top pins for security's sake. Ditto for ending a metallic thread. Put a "twee" of glue on the pins, of course, before inserting fully.

Cards: A novel idea for the ornaments which you'll be giving as gifts is to write on a tiny card (tiny in order that it not detract from your decorations): "To Kathy. Christmas 19___. From Kibby." Over the years, Kathy may end up with a bona fide collection!

(Do you save old Christmas cards? Cut out your tiny cards from the back sheet of some of these. This paper is sturdy and offers pretty colors. Ordinary paper wouldn't be very durable or attractive.)

There are several ways of attaching these tiny cards:

1.) You can simply pin the tiny card onto the ornament.
2.) String a metallic thread through a hole punched in the card, knot, string the metallic thread through the hairpin and tie a bow.
3.) Make two tiny holes in the card with your ice pick and insert your hairpin through the two holes. *After* your hairpin is through your card, inserted just a bit into the styrofoam (for the time being, keep the card at the very topmost part of the hairpin), apply glue to the part of the hairpin which is to be inserted. Let it dry for a moment. If you were to have glue on the hairpin before sticking it through the card, you would have a glue glob on your card. Now push the card down to lie flat.

When you store your decorations, use an insect spray (or mothballs) on the storage container before filling it. Moths are simply wild about all woolens, and felt, it seems, is at the top of their list!

Keep the assortment of beads which you're using in a cloth on your lap so that they're handy to pick up for beading on your wire. This cloth has another use: If you drop a bead, you won't be having to get on your hands and knees in pursuit of it. And still another use: If the telephone rings or you smell the stew scorching, you can gather up the cloth and run without incident!

So Have Fun!

In Fact, Have a Ball with a Ball!